What teachers need to know about
Learning difficulties

PETER WESTWOOD

ACER Press

First published 2008
by ACER Press, an imprint of
Australian Council for Educational Research Ltd
19 Prospect Hill Road, Camberwell
Victoria, 3124, Australia

www.acerpress.com.au
sales@acer.edu.au

Edited by Carolyn Glascodine
Cover and text design by Mary Mason
Typeset by Mary Mason
Printed in Australia by Ligare

National Library of Australia Cataloguing-in-Publication data:

Author: Westwood, Peter S. (Peter Stuart), 1936–
Title: What teachers need to know about learning difficulties / Peter Westwood.
Publisher: Camberwell, Vic.: ACER Press, 2008.
ISBN: 9780864319364 (pbk.)
Notes: Includes index.
            Bibliography.   .
Subjects: Learning disabled—Education.
            Teaching—Methodology.
            Learning disabilities.
Dewey Number: 371.9043

Contents

Preface

Students with learning difficulties comprise the largest group of students with special needs attending mainstream schools. Often our schools seem ill prepared to cater adequately for their learning needs, resulting in too many individuals leaving school without the essential literacy, numeracy and social skills they require to meet the demands of daily life. In the final report of the Inquiry into Early Intervention for Children with Learning Difficulties (*Report 30: Realising potential*) the NSW Standing Committee on Social Issues (2003) stated that these students find their schooling 'extremely alienating and dismaying' because they often find they are unable to access the supports they need to overcome or manage their difficulty, and thereby maximise their potential. The Committee concluded that, 'It is essential that current and future cohorts of children do not grow up feeling that the education system neither acknowledges nor addresses their learning needs' (p. 59).

In this book I have drawn on the international literature to explore what is known about learning difficulties and how schools can address this problem most effectively. In particular, I have focused on early identification, so that intervention and support can be provided promptly to prevent or minimise the negative affective outcomes that result from persistent failure. Often these negative outcomes operate to maintain or exacerbate a learning problem for the students concerned by impairing their self-esteem and reducing their motivation to learn.

It is not unusual to find that some students with learning difficulties also have problems with socialisation; and some have problems conforming to acceptable codes of behaviour. These problems are discussed in some detail. Most attention is given to an overview of teaching methods that work effectively for these students. Brief coverage is given to students' specific difficulties with reading and with mathematics; but this is not in depth because other books in this series address these topics in much greater detail.

It is hoped that the links to additional sources of information, together with the comprehensive list of references, will aid teachers who wish to find solutions for their students' learning difficulties.

My sincere thanks go to Carolyn Glascodine for her efficient editing and to Maureen O'Keefe for her management of the original manuscript.

PETER WESTWOOD

RESOURCES www.acer.edu.au/need2know

Readers may access the online resources mentioned throughout this book through direct links at www.acer.edu.au/need2know

Current perspectives on learning difficulties

▶ Learning difficulties are not uncommon in schools. In a few cases, they may be the result of a specific learning disability; but they are much more likely to be due to environmental factors such as social disadvantage, inappropriate curriculum, inadequate teaching, or lack of positive support for learning.

▶ Many teachers do not feel confident or competent to meet the needs of students with learning difficulties; and they tend to blame students for problems in learning.

▶ Perspectives on learning difficulties and learning disabilities vary from country to country. Prevalence rates also vary, due to differing definitions of learning difficulty and disability.

According to the Queensland Studies Authority (2007, p. 1), 'Learning difficulties refer to barriers that limit access to, participation in, and outcomes from the curriculum'. A significant number of students in our schools exhibit such difficulties for a variety of reasons. This chapter explores some of the reasons and also reports the prevalence rate for learning difficulties. In addition, several key issues associated with learning difficulties are discussed.

Defining and describing learning difficulties

Students with learning difficulties is a very general term, used widely and without much precision. Usually the term is applied to students whose learning problems in school are not directly related to any specific physical, sensory or intellectual impairment (although in some cases their intelligence may be somewhat below average). Instead, the learning difficulties may be due to external factors such as socio-cultural disadvantage, limited opportunities to learn, a lack of support from home, an inappropriate curriculum, or insufficient teaching in the early years. The learning problems these students experience are often further exacerbated by their emotional reactions to lack of success. These students, in the past, have been referred to as 'slow learners' and 'low achievers'. Badian (1996) even refers to them as having 'garden variety' learning problems, meaning that such difficulties are widespread and in no way unusual. We normally refer to these students now as having *general* learning difficulties. Their lack of success is evident across most areas of the school curriculum.

The population of students with learning difficulties also contains a very much smaller number of individuals described as having a specific learning disability (SpLD). Despite having at least average intelligence, these students experience chronic problems in learning basic literacy, numeracy and study skills. They may also have problems developing positive social relationships. The US National Center for Learning Disabilities (2001) defines a specific learning disability as:

> ... a neurological disorder that affects the brain's ability to receive, process, store and respond to information. The term 'learning disability' is used to describe the unexplained difficulty a person of at least average intelligence has in acquiring basic academic skills ... [and] LD is not a single disorder. It is a term that refers to a group of disorders.

Karande et al. (2005, p. 1029) provide a rather more detailed definition, very close to the wording of the official definition adopted in the United States of America:

> Specific learning disabilities (SpLD) is a generic term that refers to a heterogeneous group of disorders manifested by significantly unexpected specific and persistent difficulties in the acquisition and use of efficient

reading (dyslexia), writing (dysgraphia) or mathematical (dyscalculia) abilities despite conventional instruction, intact senses, normal intelligence, proper motivation, and adequate socio-cultural opportunity. The term SpLD does not include children who have learning problems that are primarily the result of visual, hearing, or motor handicaps, of subnormal intelligence, of emotional disturbance, or of socio-cultural disadvantage.

The most obvious characteristic of students with learning difficulties and learning disabilities is their failure to acquire adequate proficiency in reading and writing. Indeed, it is their problem with literacy that most commonly brings these students to the attention of teachers and parents. Very often the students' weaknesses in literacy are accompanied by similar difficulties with basic mathematics. These problems in literacy and numeracy have a negative impact on the students' progress in almost all areas of the school curriculum. Individuals with learning difficulties also seem to lack effective learning strategies for coping with the work that teachers set for them, resulting in persistently low achievement. All three areas of weakness are acknowledged in the definition of students with learning difficulties currently used in Queensland: '… those whose access to the curriculum is limited because of short-term or persistent problems with literacy, numeracy, or learning how to learn' (Department of Education, Training and the Arts, 2002a, p. 1).

In describing the typical classroom response of these students, Twomey (2006, p. 93) states:

> Many of these students avoid participating verbally during lessons, do not appear to take an interest in the subject matter, and do not perceive class discussions as learning opportunities. Their attitude serves as a defense mechanism which protects them from possible humiliation from giving the wrong answer and exposing their academic inadequacies.

According to Chan and van Kraayenoord (1998, p. 21):

> Fundamental to an understanding of learning difficulties from an information-processing perspective is the view that these students often have difficulties with collecting, interpreting, storing, modifying and retrieving information. Specifically, they fail to spontaneously activate learning strategies or previously learned information during these cognitive operations.

There is no valid behavioural or achievement checklist that helps differentiate students with general learning difficulties from those with specific learning disability. Nor need there be such a list, because all students with classroom learning problems tend to exhibit the same range of characteristics (Kavale et al., 2005). Among the most frequently identified problems are:

▶ poor attention to task and to teacher's instructions, resulting in greatly reduced time spent engaged in active learning (Whedon & Bakken, 1999)
▶ disengagement (Rowe, 2006a)
▶ low self-esteem (Lerner & Kline, 2006; McCowen, 1998; Zafiriadis et al., 2005)
▶ dysfunctional attitude (Rowe, 2006a)
▶ negative behaviours (Rowe, 2006a; Zafiriadis et al., 2005)
▶ lack of cognitive and metacognitive strategies to promote learning (Chan & van Kraayenoord, 1998; Margolis & McCabe, 2003)
▶ memory and organisational problems (Hay et al., 2005)
▶ diminished self-efficacy (Klassen & Lynch, 2007; Lancaster, 2005; Margolis & McCabe, 2003)
▶ passivity and avoidance of risk-taking (Chan & van Kraayenoord, 1998; Twomey, 2006)
▶ learned helplessness and external locus of control (Firth et al., 2007; McCowen, 1998)
▶ frustration (Watson, 2005)
▶ loss of motivation (Watson, 2005)
▶ depressive tendencies (Sideridis, 2007; Zafiriadis et al., 2005).

Gifted students with a learning disability

Liddle and Porath (2002, p. 13) state that, 'The idea that a child can be both gifted and learning disabled strikes some as a paradox'. But it is clear that some students with high intellectual potential do experience significant problems with learning basic academic skills, and can be said to have 'dual exceptionalities' (giftedness and learning disability). For example, Munro (2002) suggests that up to 30 per cent of gifted students may have problems with reading such that their attainment level is several years below expectation. Other writers have focused on their chronic difficulties in writing (e.g., Milton & Lewis, 2005).

Concern has been voiced in recent years over the plight of such students, because often they are overlooked and under-served by the system (Riggs, 1999; Stewart, 2002). In addition, students of high ability are often very acutely aware of and distressed by their difficulties, leading to secondary emotional, motivational and behavioural problems. Identification of these gifted students is essential, followed by effective remedial intervention for basic skills, and coupled with personal counselling if necessary (Lovett & Lewandowski, 2006). Stewart (2002) suggests that electronic assistive technology can be one helpful way of bypassing some of the students' problems, also enabling them to achieve some success and reveal their true abilities. Basically, these students require the same intensive and effective teaching methods recommended for use with other students with learning problems. These methods are described fully in later chapters.

Potential causes of a learning difficulty

Regardless of whether a learning difficulty is general or specific, and regardless of whether a student is gifted or average, several factors can cause difficulties in learning. Twomey (2006) suggests that there are three perspectives on learning difficulties and their underlying causes, each focusing on rather different factors and highlighting different character-istics in the students. These perspectives are referred to as (a) the *deficit model*, (b) the *inefficient learner model*, and (c) the *environment factors model*. It is probable that all three models are valid, and they are not mutually exclusive. In all three models, learning failure severely undermines a learner's self-esteem and confidence, and leads to secondary affective and motivational problems, as described in the next chapter.

Under the deficit model, it is assumed that learning difficulties are caused by cognitive and perceptual weaknesses within the student. These supposed cognitive deficits include below average intelligence, poor atten-tion to task, visual and auditory processing difficulties, weak memory capacity and inadequate comprehension of the complex language used in instructional contexts. In addition, under the deficit model, disadvantages in the student's cultural or home background, such as a dysfunctional family situation, problems associated with English as a second language, low expectations, lack of support, health problems and poverty may also contribute to difficulties in learning (Abosi, 2007).

The inefficient learner perspective does not focus on such deficits but believes the learning problem is due to an individual failing to approach school learning in a systematic way – in other words, the individual has not discovered *how to learn* effectively in school (Twomey, 2006). This model represents a more optimistic perspective for intervention because research evidence from strategy training studies suggests that students can be taught to be more effective learners (e.g., Chalk et al., 2005; Chan & van Kraayenoord, 1998; Swanson, 2000).

The third perspective considers that learning difficulties are due mainly to environmental influences, the most significant of which is the quality and appropriateness of the teaching that an individual receives (Hotchkis, 1999). Elksnin (2002, p. 252) even describes the large group of students with non-specific difficulties as 'casualties of the general education curriculum'. More will be said in a moment concerning teaching methods and curricula as possible causal factors.

Teachers' perspectives

There is still a very strong tendency for teachers to subscribe to the deficit model. They are inclined to blame students for having poor motivation or for being of limited ability. Rarely do they seek to improve the quality of their own teaching, or provide students with guidance in more effective ways of learning (Dettori & Ott, 2006; Elkins, 2007; Westwood, 1995). If teachers believe that learning difficulties are caused by innate characteristics of learners, combined with outside influences from the home and culture, there will be a general reluctance to review teaching methods or revise curriculum content (McCowen, 1998). Unfortunately, believing in the deficit model often leads teachers to lower their expectations for these students, providing them with a less-demanding, watered-down curriculum that simply adds to their frustration and alienation because their basic need for age-appropriate achievement is not being met (Frey & Wilhite, 2005; Watson & Boman, 2005).

Dettori and Ott (2006) believe that teachers tend to view underachieving students and students with learning difficulties as if they are a homogeneous group with common characteristics and needs. In general, they make very little special provision for them. In addition, they often anticipate that these students will exhibit poor behaviour in class, and this leads a teacher to focus on classroom management rather than differentiating or modifying instruction (Bakker & Bosman, 2006). Secondary school teachers in particular, are far from adept at addressing students' individual learning needs and often display a negative attitude towards students with difficulties (Watson & Boman, 2005; Watson & Bond, 2007). To improve this situation, Hunt (2004) suggests that it is essential to provide whole-school professional development for teachers in order that all staff are exposed to a wider range of teaching methods and ways of addressing individual differences.

Teaching methods and curricula

In terms of environmental influences on learning, teaching methods and school curricula can often cause or exacerbate learning difficulties. Until recently, the method of teaching was rarely investigated as a possible cause of learning difficulty. Teachers seem to assume that if something is taught (which usually means explained or demonstrated), it is automatically learned; and if it is not learned, then the problem must be due to inadequacies in the student's own ability, motivation or persistence, not to the effectiveness of the teaching method. However, not all methods of instruction are equally effective in achieving particular goals in learning. Nor are all methods equally effective with all students. Problems in learning arise if inappropriate methods are used. Examples of this are when unstructured, student-centred approaches rather than direct teaching are used in the important beginning stages of learning to read or to calculate in mathematics (DEST, 2005; Ellis, 2005). Some educators now believe that many of the problems students have with reading and mathematics are due to inappropriate or insufficient first teaching (e.g., de Lemos, 2005; Hempenstall, 2005; Hotchkis, 1999).

Other problems associated with teaching method include the teacher moving ahead too quickly with the program, devoting too little time to practice, using overly complex language when instructing and explaining, a shortage of suitable teaching materials (books, computer programs) at an appropriate level, and distracting classrooms where too many different activities are going on at the same time (Abosi, 2007). Problems also arise when the teacher does not monitor students' progress carefully day by day so is unaware when a student is experiencing difficulty. If a learning problem is not recognised early and remedied quickly, it is likely to get worse.

The curriculum itself can also be a cause of learning difficulty when the subject matter is too difficult (that is, beyond the cognitive ability level of some of the students) or the tasks and activities are boring. Anything that is too difficult or boring causes problems in holding students' attention. In fairly large classes with students of varying ability, it is not surprising that from time to time some individuals are given work that is either much too complex, or much too simple – both situations leading to frustration and disengagement. When the demands of curriculum content and learning activities are pitched too high or too low, learners may cease to learn (Paas et al., 2004). In an ideal situation, the content of the school curriculum should be challenging enough to motivate all students, but not so challenging that it causes some to become confused and discouraged. Nothing 'recedes like success' if the subject matter gets too difficult too quickly.

Prevalence of learning difficulties

Students with general and specific learning difficulties comprise the largest group of students requiring support for learning in the mainstream school context. Estimates put the prevalence rate of *general* learning difficulties at some 16 to 20 per cent of the school population (e.g., Louden et al., 2000; OECD, 2005; Zafiriadis et al., 2005), and *specific learning disability* at 3 to 5 per cent (e.g., Graham & Bailey, 2007; NHMRC, 1990; Pearl & Bay, 1999; Westwood & Graham, 2000). It is known that prevalence rates vary considerably from school to school, with some schools reporting more than 30 per cent of their students experiencing problems in learning. There is great variation also across countries in terms of the extent to which general and specific difficulties are recognised and where resources are allocated for support (OECD, 2005).

Exact prevalence figures for learning difficulties are almost impossible to ascertain because the definition of what we mean by a 'learning difficulty' is not consistent across different countries, or even across states within the same country. When teachers are asked to identify students with learning difficulties in their own classes there is often confusion about which students to include (Watson, 2005). Rivalland (2000, p. 12) comments that:

The diversity of definitions used to describe children who are deemed to have learning and/or literacy difficulties is one of the factors that complicates any analysis of how children with learning difficulties are catered for in schools ... [and] it is hard to know exactly which children we are talking about whenever policies and practices for students with learning difficulties are being described or discussed.

In an attempt to clarify the situation somewhat – and to facilitate data collection across countries – the OECD (1999; 2000; 2005) suggested three broad categories of students with special educational needs. This book is concerned with the second and third of these OECD categories.

- students with identifiable disabilities and impairments whose learning problems are attributed directly to the disability rather than to other factors
- students with learning difficulties not attributable to any disability or impairment – the learning problem is regarded as arising within the context of the teaching and learning situation
- students with difficulties due to socioeconomic, cultural, or linguistic disadvantage for whom intervention of a compensatory nature is needed.

Perspectives from home and overseas

Different countries have adopted different positions on learning difficulties and disabilities. These perspectives have resulted in somewhat different terminology and different service provision. The situations in Australia, the United States of America and the United Kingdom illustrate this point.

Australia

In Australia, the term *students with learning difficulties* includes all mainstream students who are experiencing problems in school learning, regardless of whether their difficulties are general or specific. As a consequence, writing from an Australian perspective, Graham and Bailey (2007, p. 386) state that, 'Students with learning difficulties tend to be a diverse group that demonstrates low achievement in academic subjects for a myriad of reasons'.

The preference in Australia for using the all-embracing term *learning difficulties* rather than *learning disabilities* dates back to the Cadman Report of 1976, *Learning difficulties in children and adults*. At that time, the Committee voiced doubts that a separate learning 'disability' *per se* actually existed as a phenomenon with neurological causes (Chan & Dally, 2001a; Elkins, 2000). Similar doubts have been expressed over the years in several other countries, and the existence of SpLD is still something of a contentious issue in education. In 1990, however, the National Health and Medical Research Council in Australia did differentiate between students with general learning difficulties (estimated at that time to be about 11 per cent of the school population) and students with specific learning difficulties (estimated at 4 per cent) (Hallinan et al., 1999). Queensland is the only state that has followed the NHMRC example and officially identifies students with SpLD. The position in Queensland is that:

> In all regular primary and secondary schools there are students with learning difficulties who need assistance to access the curriculum. Some of these students are experiencing short term or persistent problems in literacy, numeracy and/or learning how to learn. Some have learning disabilities. Due to the neurological basis of their difficulties, they have persistent long-term problems and may need a high level of support. These students have average to above average cognitive ability. (Department of Education, Training and the Arts, 2002b, n.p.)

The important point to note in the Australian context is that a student does not need to be labelled as 'learning disabled' in order to attract additional funding for teaching support. All students identified as having learning difficulties, regardless of type or cause, are entitled to such support. Naturally, the quantity and quality of support varies from school to school. Parent groups (e.g., SPELD) tend to argue that the needs of their children with genuine learning disabilities are not being adequately met under this system because these students require more frequent and intense tuition than is available in most schools. Often they resort to paying for private tutoring after school hours (Greaves, 2000).

Concern has been expressed about the number of students with learning difficulties and learning disabilities being identified now in Australian universities (Ryan & Brown, 2005). These are otherwise intelligent and capable individuals who are having problems with aspects of literacy and mathematics at tertiary level. It is said that learning difficulties represent the fastest growing area in university student support services, with the number of students rising by 88 per cent since 1996 (Payne & Irons, 2003).

Is this a reflection of a learning disability (dyslexia), or a reflection of inadequate teaching in their school years?

The United States of America

In the United States of America, the term *learning disability* (LD) was originally coined in the 1960s to describe students of at least average intelligence who exhibited serious difficulties in acquiring literacy and numeracy skills, and who might also have problems in areas such as perception, coordination, memory and information processing. The current US definition (one of several still circulating) is:

> [Learning disabilities are] a heterogeneous group of disorders of presumed neurological origin manifested differently and to varying degrees during the lifespan of an individual ... [and] Early indicators that a child may have LD include delays in speech and language development, motor coordination, perception, reasoning, social interaction, prerequisites to academic achievement and other areas relevant to meeting educational goals. (National Joint Committee on Learning Disabilities, 2006, p. 1)

The original expectation was that LD, as identified in students of *at least average intelligence*, would probably account for no more than 4 per cent or less of the school population. This learning disability would be recognised by a marked discrepancy between a student's measured IQ and his or her achievement level. Gradually, however, the term began to be applied to almost any student failing in the US school system regardless of intelligence level or other learning characteristics. As a consequence, the fundamental differences between students with general learning difficulties and specific learning disabilities became blurred (and remains blurred) in that country. Part of the problem arose because once students were labelled as LD they were eligible for additional services and support, whereas students with general problems in learning were not. Schools (and parents) therefore had a vested interest in seeking to have students assessed and labelled. Despite the clear and restricting definition of LD that should have applied, the number of students receiving this label grew rapidly, and continues to grow. A national survey in the United States of America reported by Altarac and Saroha (2007) suggests that LD affects 5.4 per cent of 'average' students (i.e., students with no other primary handicapping condition). However, the organisation LDonline (2008) states that *15 per cent* of the US population has some type of learning disability. Statistics from the US Department of Education (cited on the National Institute for Literacy website, 2008) reports that just over half of all students with special educational needs in US schools are students categorised as LD; and the number rose by 36.6 per cent between 1990 and 1998. So it would seem that strict application of the definition of LD in the United States of America has been virtually abandoned. Kavale et al. (2005) acknowledge the obvious over-identification of students with SpLD, indicating that many students with mild intellectual disability and with other reasons for low achievement are being included.

The United Kingdom

The United Kingdom, seemingly influenced by OECD current definitions and terminology, has clouded the issue of definition even more by adopting the terms *learning difficulty* and *learning disability* to refer to individuals with *intellectual disability* (i.e., mental handicap). In addition, while retaining the concept of specific learning disability (SpLD) for other students, the criterion of at least average intelligence has gone, thus opening up the way for over-identification. The United Kingdom currently defines SpLD in the following way:

> Pupils with specific learning difficulties have a particular difficulty in learning to read, write, spell or manipulate numbers so that their performance in these areas is below their performance in other areas. Pupils may also have problems with short-term memory, with organisational skills, and with coordination. Pupils with specific difficulties cover the whole ability range and the severity of the impairment varies widely. (Department for Education and Skills, 2003a, p. 1)

Is the concept of 'learning disability' useful?

Specific learning disability remains a controversial topic. While some experts argue strongly that, for example, a severe reading disability is qualitatively different from any of the more general forms of reading failure, others regard it as merely a different point on the same reading difficulty continuum. So, is it helpful to differentiate between general and specific learning problems?

Carlson (2005, p. 1) claims that, 'There is a vast difference between a learning difficulty and a learning disability; an individual with learning difficulty can learn using conventional teaching techniques while LD requires specialised intervention which depends on the type of disability'. It is important to challenge this claim because the intensive study of SpLD over many years has not resulted in any major breakthrough in special teaching methods or instructional resources. In terms of pedagogy, it is difficult to imagine that any teaching method found useful for students with general problems in learning to read or calculate would not also be highly relevant for other students identified as dyslexic or dyscalculic – and vice versa. If one examines the literature on teaching methodology for students with SpLD (e.g., Lerner & Kline 2006; Lewis & Doorlag 2006; Pierangelo & Giuliani 2006), one usually finds not a unique methodology applicable only to SpLD students but a range of valuable teaching strategies that would be helpful to all students. Any student with a learning problem requires assistance, and there seems little to be gained from seeking to differentiate between SpLD and non-SpLD students; the need for high-quality, effective instruction is equally strong in both groups. All students who find learning to read and write difficult are best served by designing and delivering intensive high-quality instruction, rather than by identifying them with a label (Elliott, 2008).

LINKS TO MORE ON LEARNING DIFFICULTIES

- OECD report (2005) *Students with disabilities, learning difficulties and disadvantage: Statistics and indicators.* Available online at: http://eprints.hud.ac.uk/464/
- Queensland Studies Authority (2007). *Learning difficulties.* Retrieved 21 January 2008 from: http://www.qsa.qld.edu.au/downloads/syllabus/kla_special_needs_info_learning.pdf
- A useful paper describing the 'failure syndrome' by Jere Brophy (1998) can be located online at: http://ceep.crc.uiuc.edu/eecearchive/digests/1998/brophy98.pdf

>

▶ An article 'What are learning disabilities?' by Silver (2001) is available online at: http://www.ldonline.org/article/5821.

▶ Wikipedia contains a detailed description and discussion of specific learning disability online at: http://en.wikipedia.org/wiki/Learning_disability/

▶ The terminology for learning difficulties and disabilities used in the UK is explained online at TeacherNet: http://www.teachernet.gov.uk?wholeschool/sen/datatypes/Cognitionlearningneeds/

▶ Hay, I., Elias, G. & Booker, G. (2005). Students with learning difficulties in relation to literacy and numeracy. *Schooling Issues Digest 2005/1*. Canberra: Department of Education, Science and Training. Available online at: http://www.dest.gov.au/sectors/school_education/publications_resources/schooling_issues_digest/schooling_issues_digest_learning_difficulties.htm

Affective consequences of learning difficulty

- Learning difficulties frequently bring with them a number of emotional reactions to persistent lack of success.
- Students with learning difficulties often develop low self-esteem, lose confidence in their own abilities, and develop a number of strategies for avoiding tasks that are perceived to be too challenging.
- To understand the affective outcomes from learning difficulty it is necessary to consider attribution theory, expectancy-value theory and self-efficacy theory.
- A significant component necessary in helping students with learning difficulties is to address their feelings concerning their situation, to teach them coping strategies, and to break into the failure cycle.

Where and when do learning problems begin? The answer is that for many children with learning difficulties their problems begin in the first few years of formal schooling. At this time, they are also beginning to develop important beliefs about themselves and their own capabilities. Even at an early age children can begin to regard themselves as failures in certain situations. If, for some reason, a child finds that he or she cannot do something that other children are doing easily; for example, recognising words or working with numbers – there is a significant loss of confidence and motivation. This leads in turn to deliberate avoidance of the type of activity associated with the failure, and can herald the beginning of avoidance of any new or challenging situation. Avoidance leads to lack of practice. Lack of practice ensures that the individual does not gain the relevant knowledge or skill while other children forge ahead. From that point on, the downward trajectory is set and the failure cycle begins (Robinson, 2002). The individual caught in a failure cycle thinks: 'I can't do it. I don't like it. I'm not successful. I don't have the ability. I am not going to try'. As Cross and Vidyarthi (2000, p. 13) remark, some students with difficulties are unable to separate 'failing in class' from 'failing completely as a person'. Students in this situation often develop very negative attitudes and behaviours that are detrimental to further learning. Some will exhibit unacceptable behaviours that frequently get them into trouble, while others withdraw into themselves and do not participate fully in most learning activities. Research has produced a widely agreed consensus that children who experience problems in learning tend to acquire maladaptive self-referential styles (that is, they consistently refer to themselves in a negative way) and consequently develop poor self-concept and self-esteem (Humphrey, 2002).

The effects of early failure can be long term and cumulative. Slavin (1994) reports that failure in the early school years virtually guarantees failure in later years. For example, the consequences are dire for a child who fails to learn to read in the early years. Studies have shown that children who fail to read adequately in the early years of primary school are still likely to experience major literacy problems in secondary school (e.g., Juel et al., 1986; Selikowitz, 1998; Smart et al., 2001; Torgesen, 2002). According to Hay et al. (2005), longitudinal studies have shown that 70 per cent of students with problems in literacy at age 7 still have the same problems when aged 15.

Affective factors in learning

The major affective factors associated with the learning process include:

- how much a particular learning task is valued by the learner (intrinsic motivation)
- beliefs about one's own ability to complete the task (self-esteem and self-efficacy)
- awareness of the way others may perceive you as a learner (self-worth)
- attributional beliefs concerning the causes of one's success and failure (locus of control).

These important variables tend to be strongly interrelated, with some sharing a reciprocal relationship. The experiences a student has while learning will shape, for better or worse, that student's confidence, motivation, and perceptions of his or her own capabilities – and will therefore influence future learning. When learning difficulties arise and persist they are likely to have a very detrimental impact in all four areas of affect. Burden (2002) suggests that how learners view themselves in relation to the learning situation ('learner self-perception') must be given high priority when providing support and when planning intervention programs.

The failure syndrome

An individual needs to believe that success is possible when attempting a learning task if sufficient effort is to be maintained (McNamara, 1994; Wearmouth, 2002). Students who experience lack of success in school over a long period of time begin to believe that they have no ability and will never succeed. They abandon any serious attempt to tackle the schoolwork they are set, and instead they try to find ways of preserving their status in the peer group by other methods. Often these alternative methods result in inappropriate behaviour and risk-taking.

In 1998, Brophy (p. 1) wrote:

> Failure syndrome is one of several terms that teachers commonly use (others include 'low self-concept', 'defeated' and 'frustrated') to describe students who approach assignments with very low expectations of success and who tend to give up at early signs of difficulty. [These students] often fail needlessly because they do not invest their best efforts – they begin tasks half-heartedly and simply give up when they encounter difficulty.

Similarly, Boekaerts (1996, p. 588) comments that:

> [W]hen students believe that effort will not result in mastery, they may refrain from putting in effort and settle for the belief that the subject matter is too difficult or that their personal resources are inadequate. These attributions may protect them from criticism in future, but they also trap them in a vicious circle. Indeed, students who refrain from putting in effort due to low self-efficacy lose their chances of enhancing self-efficacy, interest and self-regulation.

Lewis (1995, p. 31) reminds us:

> One of the biggest challenges for the teacher of a child who has difficulties in school-based learning is to sustain the child's confidence and enthusiasm in learning. The greatest disincentive in learning anything is to experience repeated failure. Even adults, who should be relatively confident and mature, tend to react to failure by wanting to avoid the activity which prompted the failure.

In order to understand the dynamics of the psychological factors that are associated with problems in learning, it is necessary to consider relevant attributes of a learner such as self-esteem, self-efficacy, self-worth, locus of control and motivation. It is also necessary to highlight the contribution made by attribution theory to the understanding of learned helplessness.

Self-esteem

Self-esteem can be loosely defined as appreciating one's own positive qualities and personal worth. The term self-esteem is closely allied to notions of self-concept and self-image (Santrock, 2006). Positive self-esteem is necessary for optimum mental health, and it is the responsibility of all schools to help students develop positive self-esteem. One's level of self-esteem also influences one's motivation to attempt particular tasks and meet specific challenges. Ormrod (2005) affirms that teachers need to respond to students' efforts in ways that will boost rather than lower their self-esteem.

Positive self-esteem is a by-product of doing well. Low self-esteem arises from the lack of success associated with a learning situation. All learners need to have abundant opportunity to be successful in academic, social and physical situations if they are to develop positive self-esteem and maintain good levels of motivation. In the academic domain, it is essential to gear schoolwork to students' developmental levels and capabilities, and to provide them with positive and constructive feedback. Seligman (1995) says self-esteem is created almost entirely by an individual's successes and failures in the world. Feelings of self-esteem develop as a result of meeting challenges, working successfully and overcoming obstacles.

Self-esteem is sometimes undermined in schools by practices such as:

▶ labelling certain students as failures or as problematic, either overtly in the feedback they receive or covertly by the way in which they are treated (Riley & Rustique-Forrester, 2002; Smidt, 2002)

▶ using ability-grouping within the classroom that reinforces feelings of inadequacy in those students assigned to the lowest groups (Chang & Westwood, 2001; McIntyre & Ireson, 2002)

▶ withdrawing students from classes to attend remedial lessons, because this can negatively affect the student's social status and self-esteem among peers in the regular class (West, 2002)

▶ setting difficult tasks that result in frequent failure (Chan, 1994)

▶ giving certain students simpler work in class that causes embarrassment within the peer group context (Hall, 1997).

In many ways, self-esteem in children is fairly fragile. Once it is damaged, it is extremely difficult to rebuild; but a major goal in working with students with learning difficulties is to attempt to do precisely that. Santrock (2006) suggests that there are four main ways of improving self-esteem:

▶ highlighting and building upon children's strengths, and valuing their interests

▶ providing emotional support and social approval

▶ helping children achieve by setting interesting and relevant tasks and explicitly teaching the component skills needed to complete them

▶ helping children cope successfully with challenging situations and encouraging them to reflect upon their success.

Self-efficacy

Self-efficacy is an individual's awareness of his or her personal competence in a given context. Such awareness develops over time from the individual's observation of his or her own performance and the results obtained in a variety of situations. Constructive feedback given by significant others is also influential. Achieving good results, being praised and admired by others, enjoying successes and knowing that you are doing well all contribute to the development of one's positive beliefs about self-efficacy. Conversely, poor results and too much criticism reduce self-efficacy and lower a learner's aspirations (Biggs, 1995; Gage & Berliner, 1998). Achievement and self-efficacy go hand in hand. Knowing that you are doing well enhances one's feelings of competence and confidence; and of course, the reverse is obviously true. The level of students' self-efficacy is an important variable determining how much effort they will put into any task and how long they will persist if the work is challenging (Moriarty et al., 1995). Lancaster (2005, p. 47) comments that, 'Self-efficacy beliefs contribute significantly to the level and quality of human functioning as they influence how people feel, think, motivate themselves, and behave'.

In school, a student's expectations for success when faced with a new challenge are directly related to his or her self-efficacy beliefs. Students with learning difficulties have been found to lack confidence in their own self-efficacy, particularly in relation to schoolwork (e.g., Klassen & Lynch, 2007; Lancaster, 2005). Individuals low in self-efficacy tend to shy away from difficult tasks that they see as personally threatening because they anticipate failure and loss of face among peers. Due to a history of poor outcomes from their efforts, students with learning problems tend to have very negative beliefs concerning their own self-efficacy (Ormrod, 2005).

In intervention programs, every effort must be made to try to enhance students' academic self-efficacy (Erlbaum, 2002). Setting tasks that are suitably challenging but are achievable, together with the teacher's use of descriptive praise when giving feedback are important in this respect. Descriptive praise indicates exactly why a particular outcome from effort is praiseworthy. For example, 'Well done, Marianne. You remembered to go back and check each step in the calculation. You used a very sensible approach'. When descriptive praise is perceived by children to be genuine and credible it appears to enhance their motivation and feelings of self-efficacy.

Self-worth

Self-worth is closely related to both self-esteem and self-efficacy because all three are concerned with the way individuals feel about themselves. In the context of learning difficulties, feelings of self-worth directly influence the way in which some students respond to challenges and to potential failure situations. An aspect of self-worth theory looks at the way in which we try to protect ourselves from negative evaluation by others (Eccles et al., 1998). For example, many students with learning problems would not wish their peers or the teacher to think they lacked ability in a particular area, so they would rather give the impression that when they get poor results it is because they have not put in any effort. For them, being accused of not trying is better than trying hard and being seen to fail. Self-worth theory suggests that in some circumstances a student stands to gain more by not making any effort because avoiding the task prevents any loss of face that failing would have caused. In this case, avoidance is protecting the student's feeling of self-worth (Valas, 2001). Attempting to maintain self-worth can cause a student to adopt a variety of defensive and avoidance strategies, said to be typical of students with learning difficulties.

A teacher has responsibility to strengthen all students' feelings of worth, by valuing their contributions, showing interest in them as individuals, and by using the strategies referred to above to build self-esteem and self-efficacy. Teachers must also encourage students who display defensive and avoidance tendencies to make an attempt at all the tasks they are set in class, and to give whatever guidance is necessary to make sure they succeed. It is important that teachers publicly acknowledge and praise students' positive efforts, rather than emphasising lack of effort. As a first step in working with a student with learning difficulties, it is often useful to help the student explore his or her feelings, beliefs and attitudes associated with the difficulty, and then to teach the student to use positive self-talk to overcome personal reluctance and to restore some feeling of self-efficacy. Counselling is often a necessary component of support.

Locus of control

Low confidence in self-efficacy is often accompanied by what is termed in psychology *external locus of control*. To explain the concept of locus of control, one needs to understand that individuals attribute what happens to them in a particular situation either to internal factors (e.g. their own ability, talents, effort or action) or to external factors (e.g. luck, chance, something outside their control). Children with an internal locus of control recognise that they can influence events by their own actions and they believe that they do to some extent have control over what happens to them. Appreciating the fact that outcomes are under one's personal control is a key component of feelings of self-efficacy (Pajares & Urdan, 2006). In the class-room context, an example of internality is when students recognise that if they listen attentively, ask questions, concentrate and work carefully they get much better results. Attribution theory suggests that children will not be motivated to persist in learning if they have attributed success or failure to forces over which they have no control (e.g. their own innate ability) rather than to factors they can control to some extent (e.g. the amount of effort they make, or their improved use of cognitive strategies).

Under normal circumstances, internality of control increases steadily with age. It has been found, however, that many students with learning problems and with negative school experiences remain markedly external in their locus of control in relation to school learning. They believe that their efforts in school tasks have little impact on their progress, and that what happens to them is unrelated to their own actions (Bender, 2004; McCowen, 1998). Students' positive confidence in their own capabilities rapidly erodes if they experience early failures and frustrations. Students' past causal inferences about their own successes and failures are major determinants of future motivation and achievement.

A student who remains largely external in locus of control is one who is prepared to be managed and controlled by others, such as teacher, teacher's aide, or more capable peers. There exists a vicious circle wherein the child feels inadequate, is not prepared to take a risk, seems to require additional support, gets it, and thus develops even more dependence upon others. By providing too much support, we encourage the development of learned helplessness.

The teacher's task is to break into this circle and help the student to recognise the extent to which he or she does have control over events and can influence outcomes (Galbraith & Alexander, 2005). It is natural for a teacher's aide to wish to help and support a student with learning difficulties; but this should not be done to the extent that all challenge and possibility of failure are eliminated (Fox, 2003). Failure must be possible and when it occurs children must be helped to see the causal relationship between their own efforts and the outcomes. Accepting occasional failure and *attributing that failure to the correct cause* is an essential part of learning (Seligman, 1995). As students come to understand that their mistakes often occur simply because they have not applied enough effort, or have not taken sufficient care, their perceptions of inability will decrease. Students become more internal in their locus of control, and much more involved in learning tasks, when they recognise that effort and persistence can overcome failure.

Self-efficacy is one of the important internal motivational resources needed by students (Lancaster, 2005).

An external locus of control can have a negative impact upon a student's willingness to persist in the face of a difficult task. It is easier for the students to give up and develop avoidance strategies rather than persist if the expectation of failure is high. In the instructional approach known as *attribution retraining* (McInerney & McInerney, 2006), students are taught to appraise carefully the results of their own efforts when a task is completed. They are taught to verbalise their conclusions aloud: 'I did that activity well because I took my time and read the questions twice'; 'I listened carefully, and I asked myself questions'; or 'I didn't get that problem right because I didn't check the example in the book. Now I can do it. It's easy!' The main purpose in getting students to verbalise such attribution statements is to help change their perception of the reasons for their successes or failures in schoolwork. Overtly verbalising in this way helps to focus their attention on the real relationship between effort and observed outcomes. In most cases, attributional retraining seems to have maximum value when it is combined with the direct teaching of effective strategies necessary for accomplishing particular tasks.

Learned helplessness

Low self-esteem, diminished self-efficacy, feelings of poor self-worth, and an external locus of control are all typical of the affective state termed *learned helplessness*. Students with learning difficulties resulting in low academic achievement appear to be particularly susceptible to learned helplessness. They begin to assume that anything a teacher asks them to do will be too difficult and will result in failure. This creates a serious obstacle to future learning (Valas, 2001).

Ormrod (2005), drawing on the work of several other researchers in the field, suggests that students with learned helplessness exhibit the following characteristics:

- lack of self-confidence
- tendency to set themselves easy goals and to resist challenges
- avoidance behaviour
- decreased effort

- poor concentration
- define themselves as failures
- give up easily when faced with difficulty
- underestimate their own ability
- fail to recognise their own successes when they do occur.

Once a student has developed learned helplessness, it is an uphill battle for teachers to try to reverse the process. Ormrod (2005) suggests that many of the strategies recommended for enhancing self-esteem and self-efficacy (particularly descriptive feedback, discussing reasons for failure and success, valuing students' strengths and contributions) may help to change the students' orientation. Attribution retraining, as described above, is also necessary.

Motivation

Teachers often blame a student's learning problems on his or her *lack of motivation*. It is almost as if teachers believe motivation to be a fixed and innate trait of learners, rather than a variable characteristic that is significantly influenced by outside factors. For many students with learning difficulties their problem is certainly not an innate lack of motivation but rather a marked reluctance to take risks or make any new commitment in a learning situation. This reluctance is due entirely to prior experiences of failure. Difficulties in learning significantly reduce a student's motivation, because it is hard to maintain keen interest and expend great effort in learning something if the outcome is unsatisfactory.

In classroom contexts, motivation is diminished by:

- irrelevant or boring tasks
- information overload
- lack of variety in teaching approach
- negative reinforcement and criticism
- lack of success.

Conversely, the following factors help to maximise motivation:

- interesting tasks that present the right level of challenge
- activities that bring with them pleasure, enjoyment, satisfaction and success
- social reinforcement in the form of positive feedback from others

- ownership and responsibility for a task
- freedom to make choices and decisions concerning what to do and how to do it.

Teachers need to consider the above points when seeking to regain students' interest and motivation. A large part of overcoming learning difficulties hinges on increasing students' motivation to learn. While it is ideal if motivation is *intrinsic* (that is, related to attempting a task because it is of genuine interest and worth), it is more likely that the form of motivation may have to be *extrinsic* (in the shape of incentives and rewards) in the early stages of working with students with learning difficulty.

Psychologists are interested in studying the variables that cause people to act and think in certain ways. They explore possible reasons or forces behind an individual's choice of activity, the persistence with which the person will engage in the activity, their reactions when faced with difficulties, and their thoughts about themselves as learners. Atkinson (1966) developed what is now termed the 'Expectancy-Value Theory'. This theory suggests that for students to be willing to expend personal effort on an activity, the activity and the outcome have to be seen as relevant and valuable to the learner *and* the learner has to believe he or she will be successful if attempting the task. If the learner does not feel confident about success, or if the task is not valued, very little effort will be expended and low achievement can be anticipated.

Stress and anxiety

In addition to negative impacts on self-esteem, self-efficacy and motivation, learning difficulties can also cause major anxiety and stress in students (Firth, 2006; Heiman, 2001; Zundans, 2003). In severe cases, the outcome is that the individual begins to show signs of acute depression and withdrawal (Sideridis, 2007; Zafiriadis et al., 2005). In fact, depression is reported to be fairly common among students with learning problems (Webber et al., 2002). Anxiety and depression are states that seriously impair an individual's ability to attend and concentrate in learning situations, thus compounding the original learning difficulty.

It is true, however, that certain individuals with learning difficulties seem to be remarkably resilient to such stress and anxiety, coping well with their problems and remaining in good mental health. Bryan (2003) suggests that if it is possible to identify the specific dispositions or factors that make some individuals resilient to adversity, we may be able to cultivate similar dispositions in others. Meanwhile, for many students with chronic learning difficulties it is essential to teach them effective ways of handling their stress, coping with their problems, and remaining active learners (Firth, 2006; Firth et al., 2007).

The main message in this chapter is that we need to be more sensitive than perhaps we sometimes are to the feelings, emotions, beliefs and attributions of the students we set out to help. In addition to helping them acquire essential knowledge and skills, we need to help them reflect upon and modify any negative attitudes and beliefs they may harbour concerning their own ability to improve. This is the counselling and therapeutic component of effective intervention, and it must not be neglected. Until we truly understand the *affective consequences* of learning failure, our actions to prevent such damaging occurrences for the students in our own classrooms will always be half-hearted and inadequate (McKissock, 2001).

LINKS TO MORE ON AFFECTIVE FACTORS

▶ For an overview of psychological problems associated with learning difficulty, see: http://www.schwablearning.org/articles.aspx?r=746

▶ For material on self-esteem and self-worth, see: http://www.nldline. com/self.htm and http://www.ncld.org/content/view/866/391/

▶ For a discussion of locus of control construct, see: http://wilderdom. com/psychology/loc/LocusOfControlWhatIs.html

▶ For detailed information on Albert Bandura's interpretations of self-efficacy, see: http://www.des.emory.edu/mfp/BanEncy.html

▶ For other material on self-efficacy and learning, see: http://www.des. emory.edu/mfp/self-efficacy.html

▶ Learned helplessness is the focus of a BA dissertation (2004) online at: http://www.kzoo.edu/educ/sip/2004sips/Lanser.pdf

Early identification and intervention

▶ It is essential that children with learning difficulties be identified at the earliest possible time. Appropriate intervention can then be provided.

▶ Early intervention can offset the possibility of secondary emotional reactions to prolonged failure.

▶ Early identification can involve observation and screening procedures, supplemented by information from parents and teachers.

▶ Several well-researched intervention programs are available such as *Reading Recovery*, *Success for All*, *Multilit* and *QuickSmart*.

▶ To be effective, intervention needs to be high quality, intensive and frequent.

The long-term impact of a learning difficulty can be devastating for the individual concerned, causing not only low achievement in key areas of the curriculum but also bringing with it the affective consequences discussed in the previous chapter. It is of vital importance therefore to identify children at risk of possible learning failure as early as possible in order to provide appropriate teaching to minimise the impact of a learning difficulty. There is evidence to support the view that early intervention for problems in learning in both literacy and mathematics can have extremely beneficial outcomes in terms of higher success rates in school and a reduction in the emotional problems associated with failure (Campbell & Ramey, 1994;

Dowker, 2004; Siegel & Brayne, 2005; Wasik & Karweit, 1994; Wright, 2003). The importance of providing such intervention for reading is highlighted by Sloat et al. (2007, p. 523) who state:

> Most children who do not learn to read during the primary grades will probably never learn to read well. Children who reach the end of third grade with low literacy skills typically have less access to the regular curriculum, require long-term support, and fall further behind their peers in literacy achievement and curricular knowledge.

While the identification of intellectual, physical or sensory disabilities takes place reasonably early in a child's life, the identification of less obvious difficulties in learning that are not related to a disability typically does not occur until the child is in school and already having problems (Milton, 2000). This is sometimes referred to as the 'wait to fail' model of identification and is regarded as less than satisfactory (Tollefson et al., 2007). To improve this situation many attempts have been made to identify specific signs within the developmental pattern, behaviour, or overall performance of preschool children that might be predictive of later learning difficulties. The main approaches to this problem include screening procedures and structured observation by teachers (e.g., Leung et al., 2007; Sugai & Evans, 1997; Twaddle, 2001).

Screening procedures

Most screening procedures for use with preschool children or children in the early years of schooling apply an observation checklist approach that requires teachers (and sometimes parents) to report on important aspects of children's development. These instruments focus on skills and behaviours such as speech and language development, gross- and fine-motor skills, visual and auditory perception, attention and memory that have been found in research to be predictive of success or failure in school. Sometimes screening procedures also take into account a child's work samples from kindergarten or school, and some require a child to complete certain tasks and activities that are then evaluated. Twaddle (2001, p. 26) states: 'Screening is initial assessment to support teaching and learning, and to identify areas of concern which could interfere with, or possibly restrict, a child's development and learning'.

Screening for potential learning difficulties is not a new idea. Early and current practices in identification and intervention are summarised in a comprehensive text edited by Bradley et al. (2002). Many of these screening and assessment systems are directed mainly toward predicting potential reading difficulties, but a few are now targeting mathematics (e.g., Gersten et al., 2005; Wright, 2003). The major focus has also been upon detecting specific learning disabilities rather than general learning problems; although screening in the early years can be used to reveal both.

Work on early intervention in Australia began with Helga Rowe's (1981) monograph for teachers and school counsellors. More recent work has included the *High Risk Screening Survey* (HRSS) (Sugai & Evans, 1997). This instrument covers children in from pre-primary to Grade 7 and requires a teacher to rate all children in a class in areas of academic, social and physical/sensory performance. The *Australian Kindergarten Screening Instrument* (Twaddell, 2001) is designed for children in the 4.5 to 6 years age range and covers gross- and fine-motor skills, language, pencil and paper work, reasoning and personal characteristics. In Western Australia, a project called *Catch Them Before They Fall* has explored the validity of screening for potential reading difficulties by assessing each child's phonological awareness and memory skills during the middle of the pre-primary year (Heath, 2005). Since 1995, schools in Queensland have used the *Year 2 Diagnostic Net* to monitor the progress of students in lower primary school and to identify those needing assistance in literacy and numeracy. Early identification of difficulties is also stressed in most of the action plans for literacy and numeracy prepared by all state departments of education (e.g., Government of South Australia, 2007).

In the United Kingdom, early detection of learning problems and special educational needs has been stressed for some years. Advice on this issue, for action by school-based special educational needs coordinators (SENCos), has been promulgated (Department for Education and Skills, 2002). Published instruments are also available from the National Foundation for Educational Research, such as the *Early Years Easy Screen* (EYES) (Clerehugh et al., 1991) and the *Middle Infant Screening Test* (MIST) (Hannavy, 1993).

In the United States of America, most school districts have adopted one or more forms of early screening, linked with early intervention measures for children identified as being at risk (e.g., Arkansas Department of Education, 2007; Zimmerman, 2007). Much of the research on early identification has also taken place in the United States of America.

Some of the areas of performance that are frequently included in observation checklists and screening procedures include:

- language skills (speech, vocabulary, syntax)
- auditory and phonological skills
- fine-motor skills and hand–eye coordination (as, for example, in pencil grasp, copying ability, use of scissors)
- attention and short-term memory (for example, the ability to repeat simple sentences accurately)
- writing one's own name
- comparing and matching words in print
- naming of letters and numbers.

Teacher as observer

It has been acknowledged for many years that experienced early childhood teachers are reasonably skilled in noting when young children are having learning problems. Indeed, in many ways they are at the cutting edge of the early identification process. In addition to the specific cognitive and physical skills mentioned above, preschool or first-grade teachers take into account such things as a child's ability to maintain attention to task for adequate periods of time, work without close supervision, persist with a task despite frustrations, listen to and understand instructions, socialise with peers, show interest in books and make serious efforts to learn. The contribution of these informal observations to the identification of at-risk children is as important as results from more formal testing or assessment (Flynn & Rahbar, 1998).

Information from parents

Parents can, of course, provide much important information that can help teachers or psychologists diagnose learning difficulties (Reddington & Wheeldon, 2002). Relevant aspects of a child's early development prior to beginning school and his or her behaviour patterns outside school are often known only to parents. There are risk factors such as very low birth weight, prematurity, difficult birth delivery, illnesses, accidents, anxieties and traumas that are often correlated with later learning problems (Delgado et al., 2007). Developmental achievements, such as the age at which the child could speak, walk and function independently, can also be very significant. Any information collected from parents supplements data obtained in other ways. ·

Intervention

The chief purpose of identifying children with learning difficulties at an early stage is obviously in order to intervene and provide these children with additional teaching and support. Early intervention should result in fewer children moving into middle and upper primary school with continuing problems in literacy and numeracy. In the past, intervention has usually been provided in the form of remedial teaching, with selected students withdrawn in small groups for additional teaching. This instruction has generally focused on literacy skills, with much less attention given to learning difficulties in basic mathematics (Milton, 2000). But in recent years, prevention and intervention have been reconceptualised as occurring in three tiers or 'waves' (Rohl, 2000; Tollefson et al., 2007). The 'three wave model' sees prevention and intervention in the following terms:

▸ *First wave: Prevention.* High-quality first teaching to maximise success for all children and minimise learning problems.

▸ *Second wave: Early intervention.* Small group tuition to help some children catch up. Estimated to be necessary for up to 20 per cent of children. All children still failing after this second-wave intervention require more intensive and frequent teaching represented by the third wave. It is hypothesised that children who do not respond adequately to this level of additional support are probably the students with genuine learning disabilities. The revised *Individuals with Disabilities Education Act* (IDEA) (US Department of Education, 2004) now recommends that poor response to intervention be used to identify SpLD, rather than a discrepancy between IQ and attainment. The Child Development Institute at the University of North Carolina has devised an interesting intervention approach based on rate of response to intervention (RTI) (Zimmerman, 2007) (see the Links box at the end of the chapter).

▶ *Third wave: Intensive support.* Longer-term support for individuals who do not respond quickly to second-wave tuition. Estimated to be necessary for some 5 per cent of students.

First-wave teaching

It is now generally agreed that the first-wave instruction should utilise proven, research-based teaching methods. This implies that explicit and direct instruction will be used in the early stages for teaching reading, writing, spelling and arithmetic skills, accompanied by much guided and independent practice. In the teaching of reading and spelling due attention will be given to the development of phonic skills.

In the United Kingdom this first-wave teaching takes place mainly, but not exclusively, in the daily 'literacy hour' implemented in all primary schools. Students' progress is closely monitored to identify individuals who may require additional (second-wave) teaching.

It is not essential that teachers employ particular programs or materials for first-wave teaching because effective programs can be developed from a range of suitable resources. However, examples of structured approaches and materials used by some schools in the United Kingdom and Australia for first-wave instruction in literacy include *Letterland* (Wendon, 2006), *Jolly Phonics* (Lloyd & Wernham, 1995) and *THRASS* (*Teaching Handwriting, Reading and Spelling Skills*, Davies & Ritchie, 2004). *Letterland* is a comprehensive scheme for beginners, covering phonological skills, reading, spelling and writing. It employs a synthetic phonics approach embedded within story contexts and establishes strong links between letters and sounds. Although it is a program in its own right, *Letterland* can easily be integrated into a broader language and literacy program. *Jolly Phonics* sets out to teach 42 basic sound-to-letter correspondences, using a multi-sensory approach. *THRASS* is designed to teach students how specific letters and letter groups represent the phonemes of the English language (Symons & Greaves, 2006).

Australian approaches for first-wave teaching that extend beyond phonic instruction include *SWELL* (*School-Wide Early Language and Literacy*) (Center, Freeman & Robertson, 1998), *CLaSS* (*Children's Literacy Success Strategy*) (Department of Education, Employment and Training: Victoria, 2001). *SWELL* covers children from kindergarten into the early primary years and is a code-oriented beginning reading program. It is based upon principles from the American intervention program *Success for All* (see below) and is for use within a whole class. It comprises three stages: (a) *emergent literacy* (learning about print, phonological awareness, oral language, listening comprehension); (b) *becoming literate* (phoneme awareness, phonics, spelling, comprehension); and (c) *towards literacy competence* (comprehension, writing, grammar). *CLaSS* is a whole-school approach that aims to maximise the literacy skills of all children in school years P to Grade 2 inclusive. Also relevant are the professional development materials for teachers known as *First Steps* and *Stepping Out* used in Western Australia and elsewhere (Edith Cowan University, 2007).

Second-wave teaching

Second-wave teaching continues to employ direct teaching methods and places even more emphasis on practice and mastery. The small group format enables teachers to interact with each student and to adjust instruction to each student's needs. If it is not the student's regular teacher who provides the second-wave instruction, the support teacher involved needs to maintain close liaison with the regular classroom teachers in order to link his or her instruction with the regular class program.

Specific programs for second-wave teaching include *Multilit* (*Making up lost time in literacy*) (Wheldall & Beaman, 2007), *QuickSmart* (Graham et al., 2007) and *ELRP* (*Early Literacy Research Project*) (Crevola & Hill, 1998). *Multilit* can also be regarded as third-wave intervention. It is intensive and focuses on phonic decoding, sight vocabulary and text reading for students with reading difficulties in Year 2 and above. Emphasis is placed on selecting books carefully so that they are at an appropriate instructional level for the students concerned (Pearce et al., 2006). *QuickSmart* is designed for middle school students and involves structured 30-minute sessions to be conducted by the teacher or an aide, three times per week for 26 weeks. *ELRP* is seen as a whole-school approach that targets at-risk students in the 5 to 8 years age group. The findings from this project influenced the development of the *Early Years Literacy Program* and its associated materials in the state of Victoria.

Again, *THRASS* and other code-based reading approaches are also applicable as second-wave methods (Symons & Greaves, 2006). *THRASS*, using direct teaching, is highly appropriate for students with learning difficulties who otherwise remain confused about the fact that the same sound units in English can be represented by different orthographic units (e.g. /–ight/ and /–ite/) and how the same orthographic pattern can represent different sounds (e.g. /ow/ as in *flower* or /ow/ as in *snow*).

Third-wave teaching

Third-wave teaching usually involves one-to-one or one-to-two tutoring. Children who require this level of intervention tend only to benefit if the tutoring occurs daily. The notion of providing third-wave support twice a week for 30 minutes is largely a waste of time; but unfortunately, twice-weekly sessions are all that many schools can provide. In the United Kingdom, the Department for Education and Skills (2003b) describes approaches that are appropriate for third-wave intervention, and discusses issues involved in planning and providing the prevention and intervention model in schools (see the Links box at the end of the chapter).

Reading Recovery

The most obvious example of third-wave individual intervention is *Reading Recovery* (Clay, 1993). This early intervention program was first developed in New Zealand and is now used in many other parts of the world. Children identified as having reading difficulties after one year in school are placed in the program to receive intensive one-to-one daily tuition tailored to their needs. Instruction is based on a combination of whole-language and skills-based teaching principles. Some attention is given to listening for sounds within words and practising phonic skills in context, but most attention is devoted to improving fluency. The children receive the 30-minute daily tuition for approximately 15 to 20 weeks.

A typical *Reading Recovery* lesson includes seven activities:

▶ rereading of familiar books for practice, fluency and confidence
▶ independent reading of a book introduced the previous day
▶ letter-identification activities, using plastic letters in the early stages
▶ writing of a dictated or prepared story
▶ sentence building and reconstruction from the story
▶ introduction of a new book
▶ guided reading of the new book.

The books selected for each individual are designed to give the child a high success rate. Optimum use is made of the available time and students are kept fully on task. Teachers keep 'running records' of children's oral reading performance and 'miscues', and they use this information to determine what knowledge or strategies a child still needs to learn. While *Reading Recovery* sessions have to be provided by a trained teacher, it is also evident that parent-tutors and volunteers who are often used within primary schools could easily master the basic teaching strategies.

Evidence has accumulated to indicate that *Reading Recovery* is generally effective in raising young children's reading achievement and confidence (e.g., Ng, 2006; Reading Recovery Council of North America, 2002; Smith-Burke, 2001). It is claimed that the program is highly successful with the lowest-performing children in Year 1, with at least 80 per cent of those who undergo the full series of lessons finally reading at the class average level or better. Evidence also suggests that children who participate in *Reading Recovery* are less likely to be referred later for remedial support (O'Connor & Simic, 2002). However, data from the Ministry of Education in New Zealand indicate that some 8 per cent of children in the program still have to be referred for longer-term specialist support (Ng, 2006).

Reading Recovery is not without its critics. It has been observed that skills and motivation acquired in the *Reading Recovery* lessons do not necessarily spill over into better classroom performance, possibly because the reading materials provided in the regular setting are not so carefully matched to the child's ability level, and the child receives much less individual support. Other criticisms relate to the labour-intense nature of the one-to-one intervention that places strain on school resources. Cost-effectiveness remains an unresolved issue, but Iversen et al. (2005) provide evidence to show that children can be taught in pairs, rather than individually, without any detrimental effect on their progress.

Success for All

This early intervention program from the United States of America has been adopted for use in several other countries. It involves intensive one-to-one teaching using teachers or paraprofessionals to help increase the literacy learning rate for at-risk and socially disadvantaged children (Slavin, 2004; Slavin & Madden, 2001). Lessons operate daily for 20 minutes. One unique feature of *Success for All* is that junior classes throughout the school usually work in ability groups for reading, with children going to different classrooms according to their ability level. This arrangement necessitates a block-timetabling organisation that some schools find difficult to adopt.

Chan and Dally (2000, p. 226) describe the intervention thus:

> The tutoring process in Success for All is similar to the Reading Recovery program in that its first emphasis is on reading meaningful texts. Initial reading experiences are followed by phonics instruction which provides systematic strategies for cracking the reading code. Emphasis is also given to strategies to assist and monitor comprehension.

In an attempt to overcome the reported lack of generalisation and transfer of skills, said to be found with *Reading Recovery*, the *Success for All* teachers also participate in the mainstream reading program and assist with reading lessons in the regular classroom. This helps to ensure that the one-to-one tutoring is closely linked to the mainstream curriculum, not divorced from it. Slavin and Madden (2001, p. 9) state that:

> In general the tutors support students' success in the regular reading curriculum rather than teaching different objectives. For example, the tutor generally works with a student on the same story and concepts being read and taught in the regular reading class. However, tutors seek to identify learning problems and use different strategies to teach the same skills. They also teach metacognitive skills beyond those taught in the classroom program.

Research evidence in general has been very supportive of *Success for All* as an effective intervention model (Morrow & Woo, 2001). However, a few students with learning disabilities appear to require even more intensive instruction.

Involving parents in intervention

To be maximally effective, intervention in schools needs to be extended into the home if possible. When parents support their child's literacy and numeracy skills at home, much is achieved by reinforcing work from school and providing additional practice. Fielding-Barnsley and Purdie (2003) report very positively on the outcomes from what they term a 'dialogic approach' in which parents are trained to interact positively with their children (age 6+ years) in a literacy learning context at home.

They are encouraged to read to the children, discuss stories, play games or activities to develop awareness of sounds in words, rhyming and alliteration (phonological awareness), and teach the alphabet and basic phonics.

General principles for intervention

Over recent years a consensus has emerged over the essential ingredients needed for successful intervention for learning difficulties. It seems from firsthand observation and from research that the following general principles need to be incorporated in all forms of early intervention:

- Children experiencing difficulties in learning must spend considerably more time receiving direct help and guidance from teachers and parents.
- Frequent successful practice is essential to build skills to a high level of automaticity.
- Daily instruction will achieve very much more than twice-weekly intervention.
- The instruction provided in intervention programs must be of a very high quality and delivered with clarity and intensity.
- In order to ensure intensity and frequency of intervention, at-risk children need to be taught individually for part of each day, graduating later to small groups and to in-class support, before independent progress in the regular class becomes viable.
- As well as attempting to improve basic academic skills, early intervention must also focus on correction of any negative behaviours such as poor attention to task or avoidance that are impairing the student's progress.
- Although withdrawing a student for individual or group work can achieve a great deal, it is also essential that the regular classroom program be adjusted to allow at-risk children a greater degree of success in that setting. Failure to adapt the regular class program frequently results in loss of achievement gains when the student no longer receives assistance.
- There is a danger that children with learning problems may receive a remedial program containing too many decontextualised skill-building exercises. All work must be interesting and meaningful, and there must be genuine reasons for engaging in the activities provided in an intervention.
- The materials used with at-risk children must be carefully selected to ensure a very high success rate. For teaching early reading, repetitive and predictable texts are particularly helpful.

▶ Multi-sensory and multimedia approaches often help children with learning difficulties attend, assimilate and remember particular units such as letter–sound correspondences, sight vocabulary and spellings.

▶ Children should be taught explicitly the knowledge, skills and strategies necessary for identifying words, extracting meaning from text, spelling, writing and calculating with numbers.

▶ Writing should feature as much as reading in early literacy interventions. Concepts about print can be acquired through writing as well as reading, and a great deal of phonic knowledge can be developed through helping children work out the sounds they need to use when spelling words.

▶ In tutoring for mathematics improvement, due time and attention must be given to developing automaticity in computational skills, as well as applying taught strategies for problem solving.

▶ The use of other tutors (aides, volunteers, peers, parents) can be very helpful. These individuals need to be taught how to function effectively in the tutor-supporter role.

▶ Maximum progress occurs when parents or others can provide additional support and practice outside school hours.

Benefits and pitfalls of intervention

It is always said, for good reason, that children with learning problems need to be identified and helped as soon as possible. In general, that advice is obviously sound because prevention is much more effective than attempting a remedy after major problems have arisen. However, what is not always so readily appreciated is that the very act of intervention inevitably labels some students as 'different' within the school system and within their own eyes (e.g. 'I am a child at risk', 'I am a remedial student', 'I am a Reading Recovery child', 'I need a support teacher', and so forth) and places them in a sub-system that changes their school experience compared to that of other students (Lewis, 1995). The child who is withdrawn from class or receives additional attention in the classroom does feel different (and perhaps inferior) and is viewed as different by peers. Valas (2001) reports that being placed within a special education support service, or having contact with a psychologist, special education teacher, or therapist can have a detrimental effect on the self-esteem of students with learning difficulties. Making children feel different or 'deficient' can cause negative affective outcomes.

The potentially negative effect of identification and intervention creates a significant dilemma for schools. How can additional support best be provided? How do you provide assistance without making it obvious that you are doing so? Is this more of a problem at secondary school than primary school? According to studies by Klassen and Lynch (2007), adolescents want help to be *discreetly* provided. But, how can a school provide an unobtrusive form of support that still has sufficient intensity, frequency and duration to have any real benefit? These dilemmas remain unresolved. Perhaps any skill-development benefits for a student resulting from high-profile intervention outweigh negative impacts stemming from the identification and labelling process. This important issue is addressed further in the final chapter, where affective outcomes from the practice of 'differentiation' are explored.

LINKS TO MORE ON IDENTIFICATION AND INTERVENTION

▶ The topic of identification of SpLD through children's response to intervention is addressed by Tollefson, J. M., Mellard, D. F. & McKnight, M.A. (2007). *Responsiveness to intervention: A SLD determination resource.* The US National Research Center on Learning Disabilities, Information Digest (Winter issue 2007). Available online at: www.nrcld. org/resource_kit/general/RTIdigest2007.pdf

▶ A good example of kindergarten assessment in relation to identifying SpLD can be found at the Arkansas Department of Education (Special Education) website in the *Resource guide for specific learning disabilities* (2007). Available online at: http://arksped.k12.ar.us/ documents/stateprogramdevelopment/DyslexiaGuideApril30.pdf

▶ A document prepared by the National Joint Committee on Learning Disabilities (2005) presents a clear statement on the concept of 'responsiveness to intervention'. Available online at: http://www. ldonline.org/article/11498. The Committee also provides a statement on 'learning disabilities and young children: identification and intervention' (2006), online at: http://www.ldonline.org/article/11511

>

- A very comprehensive summary of what teachers should look for when identifying potential learning difficulties at preschool, primary and secondary school levels is provided by Bergert (2003) *The warning signs of learning disabilities.* ERIC Digest online at: http://www.ericdigests. org/2001-4/ld.html

- A brief summary article, Lyon, G. R. & Fletcher, J. M. (2002). *Early identification, prevention, and early intervention for children at risk for reading failure.* Center for Development and Learning, online at: http://cdl.secured-ecommerce.net/resource-library/articles/strategies. php?id=19&type=author

- A comprehensive summary of intervention principles and practices in Australia can be found at the website of the Australian Government Department of Education, Employment and Workplace Relations, online at: http://www.dest.gov.au/sectors/school_education/publications_ resources/other_publications/successful_programs_strategies_for_ children.htm

- Brooks (2002) provides an evaluation of intervention methods for literacy in use in the UK at this time. His review includes some approaches that are also used in Australia and New Zealand (e.g., *THRASS*, Reading Recovery). Available online at: http://www.dfes.gov. uk/research/data/uploadfiles/RR380.pdf

- A similar review covering mathematics interventions (Dowker, 2004) is available online at: http://www.dfes.gov.uk/research/data/uploadfiles/ RR554.pdf

- See also Department of Education and Skills (UK) (2003). *Targeting support: Choosing and implementing interventions for children with significant learning difficulties.* Retrieved 28 January 2008 from: http:// www.standards.dfes.gov.uk/primary/publications/literacy/63437/nls_ chooseintervent_020103.pdf

- Details of screening tests and other early identification instruments can be found in the catalogues of the National Foundation for Educational Research in the UK and from the Australian Council for Educational Research.

- For details of the *SWELL* literacy approach, see: http://www.uranpoinss. qld.edu.au/pages/swellweb6.htm

- For information on *CLaSS* and *ELRP*, see Hill, P. W. & Crevola, C. A. (n.d.). Key features of a whole school, design approach to literacy teaching in schools. Available online at: http://www.bsw.vic.edu.au/ EarlyYears/researchpage_files/hillcrev_3.pdf
- Details of the Australian early literacy program *An even start*, introduced in 2008 to assist children who did not reach the national literacy benchmarks, can be visited at: http://www.anevenstart.dest.gov.au

four

Social and behavioural issues

KEY ISSUES

▶ Studies over many years have revealed that students with learning difficulties often have significant problems making friends and being accepted by peers.

▶ Direct intervention is necessary to assist some students with learning difficulties to develop socially.

▶ Training in social skills is important; but research findings suggest that it is not always effective.

▶ Students with learning difficulties may exhibit behavioural problems that must be addressed appropriately by teachers.

▶ Attention deficit hyperactivity disorder (ADHD) contributes to learning and behavioural problems in some students.

It is well established that many students with learning problems also have difficulty in developing positive social relationships with their peers and with their teachers (Pavri & Monda-Amaya, 2001). Overwhelming evidence confirms that many students with learning difficulties have significant deficits in social skills and in communication competence that may predispose them to negative interactions with their peers (Donahue & Pearl, 2003; Kavale & Forness, 1996; Pearl & Bay, 1999; Vaughn et al., 1993). Bryan (1998) suggests that almost 60 per cent of SpLD students experience problems of being ignored, isolated, or rejected by classmates. In addition, some students with learning problems may become victims of teasing and bullying. The situation is most problematic for students who also have an emotional or behavioural disorder; and there is a danger that such students become marginalised or are openly rejected by classmates. Wiener (2002) reports that many students with learning difficulties have major problems with social relationships and exhibit a variety of emotional reactions.

Students are at risk in school if they lack social skills, are aggressive or provocative, and are rejected or victimised by others (Fox & Boulton, 2005; Yuen et al., 2007). It is for this reason that helping these students establish better social relationships with others is one of the most important goals in their education. It is evident that poor peer relationships during the school years can have a lasting detrimental impact on quality of life, on mental health, and on social and personal competence in later years.

It is essential that teachers are alert to the potential social development problems that students with learning difficulties may have, and are prepared to intervene with specific support. In an ideal world, teachers and caregivers would identify any social adjustment problems students are having and would attempt to intervene in some way to help them acquire necessary social skills. But it is not an ideal world, and although some studies have shown that mainstream teachers are aware of the fact that students may have problems in social functioning (e.g., Tur-Kaspa, 2002) other evidence suggests they often do not recognise the extent of the student's social difficulties and therefore do not intervene to improve matters (Hutchinson et al., 2002).

Problematic social development

Studies have confirmed that students with learning difficulties are often less accepted, more openly picked upon, or more neglected socially than their classmates (Fry & Bartak, 2006; Pearl & Bay, 1999; Valas, 1999). In a review of the relevant research literature, Coleman and Byrd (2000, p. 302) suggest that, 'most victimised children do not have the requisite general social competencies (friendliness, cooperativeness, prosocial skills, sense of humour) for becoming esteemed members of the peer group'. Humphrey (2002, p. 30) states that, 'Children with learning difficulties, whether specific or general, are at an increased risk for bullying and teasing, and are less likely to be accepted by their peer group'.

Riddick's (1996) interviews with dyslexic students revealed that personal shame, embarrassment, depression and anger were common reactions to their failures, and at least half the group reported being teased about their difficulties by the peer group. Similarly, an earlier study by Martlew and Hodson (1991) found that students with SpLD were teased significantly more often than students without SpLD, and had problems in establishing friendships. Evidence has accumulated over the years that students with low achievement, particularly those of average intelligence with a specific learning difficulty, are often targets of various forms of peer victimisation (Mishna, 2003; Norwich & Kelly, 2004; Pearl & Bay, 1999). It is suggested that often there are characteristics of these students that make them vulnerable; for example, they may appear to be weaker, shy, nervous, or socially inept (Mishna, 2003; Okabayashi, 1996). On the other hand, they may display irritating, aggressive and provocative behaviours that cause other students to dislike them. Often there is something about their behaviour that seems to contribute to their vulnerability (Fried & Fried, 2003). It is noticeable that most of the personal and behavioural characteristics reported to be typical of students who are socially rejected or bullied by others (e.g. passivity, feelings of inadequacy, self-blame, poor self-concept, diminished self-esteem, problematic peer relations and external locus of control) are also characteristic of students with learning difficulties (Gans et al., 2003; Mishna, 2003). They often see themselves as failures, and regard themselves as stupid and powerless (Harris & Petrie, 2003).

This chapter presents some of the steps that can be taken to facilitate positive social interaction and to reduce troublesome behaviour that may cause a student to be disliked by other students. To enhance social development, teachers must create classroom environments where competition is not a dominant element and they must use activities that encourage cooperation among students (Johnson & Johnson, 2003). They may also need to teach certain students the social skills they seem to lack (Seevers & Jones-Blank, 2008).

A supportive classroom environment

A positive and supportive environment is essential for the social development of all students. To facilitate social interaction, three conditions are necessary:

▶ The general attitude of the teacher and the peer group towards students with learning problems must be as positive and accepting as possible.

▶ The environment should be arranged so that students with learning difficulties have the maximum opportunity to become socially involved in group or pair activities in the classroom and during recess in the schoolyard.

▶ Some students with significant socialisation problems need to be taught the specific pro-social skills that may enhance contact with peers.

Peer-group members can be encouraged to maintain and reinforce social interactions with less able or less popular students. Often they are unaware of the ways in which they can assist. Enlisting the help of the peer group can be achieved through a system called *Circle of Friends*. This is a support strategy to help students who have difficulty finding a friend and coping with work in class (Barrett & Randall, 2004). The approach originated in Canada but is now used in the United States of America, the United Kingdom and Australia as one way to foster social inclusion for students with difficulties. *Circle of Friends* operates by involving some of a student's classmates as natural supporters to help the child acquire more positive behaviours and cope with schoolwork routines and assignments.

To increase the chances of positive social interaction for students with learning difficulties, a teacher could make more frequent use of non-academic tasks (e.g. games, model-making, painting) because these place the child in a situation where he or she can more easily fit in and contribute. In addition, 'peer tutoring' and 'buddy systems' have been found effective. Several versions of these exist, including *Classwide Peer Tutoring* (CWPT) involving all students. Research over two decades has confirmed the effectiveness of peer tutoring for improving learning outcomes for students at all age and ability levels (McMaster et al., 2006).

Cooperative and collaborative activities

Regular use of group work in the classroom is one way of providing students with opportunities to develop social skills and learning skills through collaborating with others (Knight et al., 2004). Careful planning is required if group work is to achieve the desired educational and social outcomes. The size of a group is important, and students working in pairs is often a good starting point. The composition of groups is also important in order to avoid obvious incompatibility between students' personalities. Group members may have to be taught how to work together productively (Yamanashi, 2005). They may need to be shown behaviours that enable cooperation – listening to the views of others, sharing, praising each other and offering help to others. If the task involves the learning of specific curriculum content, the students need to be shown how to rehearse and test one another on the material.

Initially there is some merit in having groups of students working cooperatively on the same task at the same time. This procedure makes it much easier to prepare resources and to manage time effectively. Choice of tasks for group work is very important. Tasks have to be selected which *require* collaboration and teamwork. It is not enough merely to establish groups and to set them to work. The ways in which individual tasks are allotted need to be carefully planned (division of labour), and the way in which each student can assist another must also be made clear. Teachers should monitor closely what is going on during group activities and must intervene when necessary to provide suggestions, encourage the sharing of a task, praise examples of cooperation and teamwork, and model cooper-ative behaviour themselves. Doveston and Keenaghan (2006) suggest that there is great value in discussing openly with a class the best ways of making group work effective, and explicitly identifying the skills necessary to cooperate productively with others.

The frequent use of collaborative groupwork creates a necessary but not sufficient condition for some students with learning difficulties to improve their social interactions with others. In the case of students displaying extreme withdrawal or rejection, simply relying on classroom interactions is not always sufficient. Sometimes it is necessary for a student to be removed from the classroom, counselled and coached intensively in particular social skills before those skills can be applied in the group setting.

Teaching social skills and strategies

Social skills comprise a set of competencies that allow children or adolescents to initiate social interactions with others, establish their acceptance in the peer group, and cope effectively and adaptively with their social environ-ment. As stated above, some students with learning difficulties and with emotional and behavioural problems are particularly at risk of social isolation

(Gresham, 2002) – although it is important to stress that some students with learning difficulties do not have a socialisation problem and are actually popular with classmates, particularly if they have a pleasant personality. One of the main reasons why certain students are unpopular is that they lack appropriate social graces that might make them more acceptable.

Cartledge (2005) recommends that social skills instruction should begin in the preschool or primary years, when children are most receptive to behaviour change. Early training in social skills can be instrumental in reducing or preventing problems in later years. Cartledge also advises that social skill instruction should be embedded in the context of events that occur naturally within the children's own classroom setting. Research shows that there is very limited transfer or maintenance of skills when they are taught in contrived exercises unrelated to the real classroom. The most meaningful settings in which to enhance a child's skills are usually the classroom and schoolyard. The skills to be targeted need to be of functional value to the child in the social environment in which he or she operates.

Most programs for training social skills are based on a combination of modelling, coaching, role-playing, rehearsing, feedback and counselling. In each individual case, the first step is to decide what the priorities are for this student in terms of specific skills and behaviours to be taught.

Social skills training usually includes the teaching of some or all of the following behaviours:

- making eye contact
- greeting others by name
- gaining attention in appropriate ways
- talking in a tone of voice that is acceptable
- initiating a conversation
- maintaining conversations
- answering questions
- listening to others and showing interest
- sharing with others
- saying please and thank you
- helping others
- making apologies when necessary
- joining in a group activity
- taking turns
- smiling at others

▶ accepting praise
▶ giving praise
▶ accepting correction without anger
▶ coping with frustration
▶ managing conflict.

To a large extent these behaviours, once established, are likely to be maintained by natural consequences – that is, by a more satisfying interaction with peers. Individuals with acceptable social skills are less likely to engage in problem behaviour, are better at making friends, are able to resolve conflicts peacefully, and have effective ways of dealing with persons in authority (Poulou, 2005).

As well as having appropriate positive pro-social skills, a socially competent individual must also *avoid* having negative behavioural characteristics that prevent easy acceptance by others; for example, high levels of irritating behaviour (interrupting, poking, shouting), impulsive and unpredictable reactions, temper tantrums, abusive language, or cheating at games. In many cases these undesirable behaviours may need to be eliminated by behaviour modification or through cognitive self-management.

Some researchers warn against over-optimism in regard to the long-term efficacy of social skills training (e.g., Kavale & Mostert, 2004; Maag, 2005). While most social skills training produces positive short-term effects, there are usually major problems with maintenance and generalisation of the trained skills over time (Cartledge, 2005). Training in social skills is not a matter of simply teaching a student something that is missing from his or her repertoire of behaviours, but rather involves *replacing* an undesirable behaviour that is already strongly established with a new alternative behaviour. The negative behaviours we often take as indicative of lack of social skill in some students (e.g. non-compliance) may actually be useful behaviours for the individual concerned if they achieve desired outcomes such as avoiding work that the individual finds threatening, or gaining them more attention than they would otherwise receive (Hudson, 2003).

Addressing behavioural problems

Behavioural problems can arise because of stresses or difficulties a student is experiencing in life outside school. In such cases, the problem behaviour causes the learning difficulty and low achievement because the student is preoccupied with worries and is often in trouble. Causal factors outside school, for example in the family situation, are difficult for teachers to deal with in any practical sense, but teachers should adopt an understanding attitude toward students in this situation and perhaps make reasonable allowances rather than adding to their problems by harsh discipline. School counsellors and social workers have an important role to play both in providing support to the student and in keeping teachers informed of the background difficulties.

In a few cases, the problem behaviours may be due to a student's inability to communicate effectively (Tait, 2007). Aggressive behaviour is sometimes the result of students' inability to be verbally assertive and to win an argument or have their opinion heard. Instructions from the teacher may not be understood, and the student becomes frustrated and angry.

But it is clear from what has been said so far, that inappropriate and challenging behaviour from a student with learning difficulties can be directly caused by the student's inability to cope with schoolwork successfully. In other words, in such cases the learning difficulty is the primary cause of the problem behaviour. Inappropriate behaviour then creates a situation where much of the teacher's time is taken up with managing or correcting the behaviour rather than providing effective teaching and encouragement for the student (Hudson, 2003; Shanahan & Richmond, 2007). All too often teachers react overtly to undesirable behaviour, thus reinforcing it. Instead of ignoring or deflecting inappropriate behaviour, teachers often reinforce the behaviour unintentionally by reacting overtly to it. In such situations the student's learning opportunities are further compromised. Students who are constantly seeking attention, interrupting the flow of a lesson and distracting other students are often very troubling to teachers (Bakker & Bosman, 2006). Frequent disruptions have a ripple effect and can cause major reduction in the overall quality of learning and teaching occurring in that classroom, as well as destroying a positive classroom atmosphere. It is reported that teachers can lose about half of their teaching time in some classrooms due to students' disruptive behaviour (Charles & Senter, 2005).

Naturally, teachers feel professionally threatened by students who constantly challenge their control. The feeling of threat can cause the situation to get out of hand, and a teacher can get trapped into confrontations with a student, rather than looking for possible solutions that will provide responsible choices and save face for the student and teacher (Lindberg et al., 2005). Inappropriate behaviour in the classroom is often inadvertently rewarded by the teacher's response to it. For example, a teacher who spends a lot of time reprimanding students who misbehave is in fact giving them a lot of individual attention (social reinforcement) at a time when they are behaving inappropriately. This misapplication of reinforcement encourages the very behaviour the teacher is trying to prevent.

The traditional approach to behavioural problems in school has tended to be reactive and aversive rather than preventive. However, in recent years there has been a shift toward a more positive behaviour support model (PBS) that attempts to be proactive by reducing the likelihood that serious problems will arise (Allen et al., 2005; Barton-Arwood et al. 2005; Bryer et al., 2005). PBS intervention strategies include:

▶ modifying or eliminating classroom conditions that increase the probability of challenging behaviour arising (for example, by reducing group size, intro-ducing alternative materials or assignments, arranging seating differently, eliminating interruptions and distractions, establishing routines for distributing materials)
▶ 'catch them being good': positive reinforcement rather than reprimands ('Well done, Green Group. You are working very hard')
▶ discussing behaviour codes and personal rights and responsibilities with students
▶ explicitly teaching students behaviours they need to display to meet the teachers' expectations
▶ teaching students self-monitoring and self-control strategies
▶ providing active and supportive supervision.

Teachers may also use strategies such as deflection and diffusion to take the heat out of a potential confrontation. Teacher: 'Aaron, I can see you're upset. Cool off now and we'll talk about it later; but I want you to start work now please'. The judicious use of humour can also help to defuse a situation, without putting the student down. Compliance with a teacher's instructions may be improved by presenting a sequence of three or four simple requests that have a high probability of being complied with before giving the instruction that may be resisted. The 'momentum' of complying with the easy requests carries over into compliance with the final instruc-tion (Stephenson, 2006).

Corrective actions a teacher might decide to use for low-level inappropriate behaviour include:

▶ tactical ignoring (non-reinforcement) of the student and the behaviour

▶ simple directions ('Sharon, get back to your work please')

▶ question and feedback ('What are you doing, Michael? OK, That's good')

▶ rule reminders ('Jeanne, you know our rule about noise. Please work quietly')

▶ simple choices ('Excuse me, Ben. You can either work quietly here, or I'll have to ask you to work on your own at the carrel – OK?').

When inappropriate behaviour is more extreme and causing disruption to others, a teacher will need to take stronger action such as isolating a student from the class group by using 'time out'. However, Hudson (2003) reminds us that this form of discipline is rarely effective in the long term, although it may solve an immediate discipline problem.

If a behavioural problem is persistent, it becomes increasingly important that the teacher (and/or the behaviour management team in the school) should analyse possible reasons for this behaviour and examine the context in which the learning and behaviour problems are occurring (Lancaster, 2005). The analysis deals with issues that are immediately observable in the classroom. For example, it is pertinent to ask:

▶ How frequently is this behaviour occurring?

▶ When does the behaviour occur?

▶ When is the behaviour *least* evident?

▶ How is the class organised at the time (groups, individual assignments, etc.)?

▶ What is the teacher doing at the time?

▶ How is the student occupied at the time?

▶ What is the teacher's immediate response to the behaviour?

▶ What is the student's initial reaction to the teacher's response?

▶ How do other students respond to the situation?

▶ What strategies has the teacher used in the past to deal successfully with a similar problem?

It is not only externalising behaviour such as aggression, anger, vandalism and bullying that need to be modified. It is equally important that students who have reacted to learning failure by withdrawing into themselves and becoming passive and anxious should also receive attention. Unfortunately, they are less likely to be noticed by their teachers because they present no problem to the management of the class. Nor is it easy to restore a student's confidence and assertiveness. This will only occur if the individual becomes more successful in schoolwork and is openly accepted and valued by the teacher and the peer group for his or her other strengths.

It must be recognised that changing a student's behaviour is often very difficult. The behaviour we regard as inappropriate has proved to be quite effective for the student in attaining certain personal goals (e.g. escape from an unpleasant task; getting the teacher's full attention). The behaviour has been practised frequently and has become very well established. In order for a positive behaviour change to occur, the student must first *desire* to change. The responsibility of the teacher is then to help the student understand exactly *how* to bring about and maintain the change. The student needs to replace inappropriate behaviour with more appropriate and positive behaviour (Hudson, 2003). Attention must also be given to improving the student's self-monitoring and decision making in order to increase self-control over the problem behaviour.

The main goal of any type of behaviour-change intervention should be the eventual handing over of control to the individual concerned, so that he or she is responsible for managing the behaviour. One way of achieving this is to employ cognitive behaviour modification (CBM). This intervention first helps the student analyse the inappropriate behaviour and understand that the response (e.g. lashing out at others, arguing with staff) is not helping in any way. The student is then taught to use 'self-talk' to help monitor his or her own reactions to challenging situations when they occur. For example: 'OK. Stay calm. Read the question carefully. Read it again. Do I understand this? No. I must put up my hand and ask the teacher to explain it for me'. The self-talk enables the student to process aspects of the situation rationally and enables him or her to control and manage responses more effectively. A key ingredient in the approach is teaching the student to use self-talk statements that serve to inhibit impulsive and inappropriate thoughts or responses, allowing time for substitution of more acceptable responses; for example, to be assertive but not aggressive.

Attention-deficit hyperactivity disorder

One detrimental behavioural pattern that is fairly often associated with learning difficulties, either as a primary cause of the difficulty or as an additional problem, is hyperactivity. Some students with learning problems display a need for excessively high levels of physical activity. This causes them to have great difficulty remaining in their seats and keeping still. They twitch and wriggle, they drum their fingers on the desk, they bounce their feet, they poke other students, they pick things up and then drop them, and they want to move around the room frequently. They do not seem able to inhibit impulsive actions or responses. It is believed that in some cases this problem of hyperactivity has a physical cause and is not simply due to lack of self-control.

In almost all cases of hyperactivity the student also has significant difficulty in maintaining attention to task, and is highly distractible and distracting in learning situations. For this reason, the condition is now referred to as *attention-deficit hyperactivity disorder* (ADHD). This condition is recognised fully in the *Diagnostic and statistical manual of mental disorders* (4th ed., APA, 2000), an official source of reference for psychologists. It is considered that approximately 3–5 per cent of school-age children present symptoms of ADHD (Rappley, 2005), but the classification ADHD is often misused and applied to students who are merely bored and restless, or who are placed in a class where the teacher lacks good management skills. Hyperactivity is also present sometimes as an additional problem in certain disabilities (e.g. cerebral palsy, acquired brain injury, specific learning disability and emotional disturbance).

Students with ADHD, while not necessarily below average in intelligence, usually exhibit poor achievement in most school subjects (Lucangeli & Cabrele, 2006). Impaired concentration and restlessness associated with ADHD seriously impair a student's learning capacity. The literature indicates that most hyperactivity diminishes with age even without treatment, but in a few cases the problems persist into adult life. Treatments have included diet control, medication, psychotherapy, behaviour modification and cognitive behaviour modification. According to Lerner and Kline (2006), the most effective treatment for ADHD requires the integrated use of effective teaching strategies, a behaviour management plan, parent counselling, a home management program and medication.

Students with ADHD need to be engaged as much as possible in interesting work, at an appropriate level, and in a stable environment. Enhancing the learning of students with ADHD will also involve:

- providing strong visual input to hold attention
- using computer-assisted learning (CAL)

▶ teaching the student better self-management and organisational skills

▶ monitoring the student closely during lessons and finding many opportunities to praise them descriptively when they are on task and productive.

To minimise the effect that ADHD has on academic progress, it is particularly important to increase the amount of work these students complete each lesson. This often requires a structured program with regular and immediate rewards for work completion and goals achieved (Wright, 2007).

LINKS TO MORE ON SOCIAL AND BEHAVIOURAL ISSUES

▶ *LDonline* website has useful links to several articles on behaviour and social skills. Available online at: http://www.ldonline.org/indepth/behavior

▶ *LDonline* also has a relevant item by Mather and Goldstein on behaviour modification. Available online at: http://www.ldonline.org/article/6030

▶ *Internet Special Education Resources* website has a comprehensive paper by Adam Cox (2006) on teaching social skills. Available online at: http://www.iser.com/teaching-social-skills.html

▶ *Positive Behavioral Interventions and Supports* website provides comprehensive coverage on the topic of positive behaviour support, with links to several recent articles. Available online at: http://www.pbis.org/schoolwide.htm. See also: http://www.pbis.org/main.htm

▶ Cognitive behaviour modification applied to social skills training is the topic of an article by Smith, S. W. (2002) in *ERIC Digests* online at: http://www.ericdigests.org/2003-3/skills.htm

▶ The National Institute of Mental Health website (2008) provides a concise overview of ADHD. Available online at: http://www.nimh.nih.gov/health/topics/attention-deficit-hyperactivity-disorder-adhd/index.shtml

five

Teaching students with learning difficulties

KEY ISSUES

▶ Research has shown clearly which teaching methods produce the best results for students who have learning difficulties. Unfortunately, these methods are not widely used by classroom teachers.

▶ Much is known about effective instruction that can reduce failure rates. But teachers-in-training are not specifically exposed to this research and they are encouraged to use student-centred approaches.

▶ Learning to read is problematic for students with learning difficulties. Effective methods for teaching reading are known and should be used.

▶ Effective methods for teaching mathematics are required to prevent the high failure rate that is common in this subject.

In Chapter 1, attention was drawn to the fact that many learning difficulties are caused or exacerbated by inappropriate teaching methods. Due to the fairly disappointing standards achieved by too many students in recent years there have been demands in several countries for schools to adopt teaching methods that have been carefully evaluated for their efficacy, rather than employing methods based on teachers' personal intuition, style, or preference (e.g., DEST, 2005; Moran, 2004). Recent emphasis on the importance of evaluating the effectiveness of methods of instruction before they are adopted for widespread use in schools applies not only to methods used for general teaching purposes but also those used for remedial intervention (Wheldall, 2007).

In the past, some educators have suggested that student-centred constructivist approaches such as activity methods, project work, resource-based learning, discovery maths and whole-language approach to literacy have most to offer students with special educational needs (e.g., Goddard, 1995; Kroll, 1999; MacInnis & Hemming, 1995). These approaches often emphasise social interaction more than mastery of curriculum content, and are deemed to be more accommodating of differences among students. However, research evidence does not support this viewpoint (Swanson & Deshler, 2003; Vaughn et al., 2000). Student-centred approaches require much more initiative, persistence and independent learning ability than most students with learning difficulties possess (Kirschner et al., 2006; Mayer, 2004).

What has research said about teaching methods?

The evidence clearly indicates that students with learning difficulties make best progress in academic subjects under teaching methods that are direct, explicit and well structured (Ellis, 2005; Mastropieri & Scruggs, 2002; Rowe, 2006a; Swanson & Deshler, 2003). They do less well with methods that are unstructured, open-ended, and rely on incidental learning through activity and discovery (Carnine, 2000; de Lemos, 2004; Mastropieri et al., 1997; Pincott, 2004). This finding applies particularly to the beginning stages not only of reading, writing and mathematics but also subjects such as science, geography, technology and other skills-based and knowledge-based areas of the curriculum. Wilen et al. (2000) comment that research shows that a systematic approach has benefits for young children, students with learning difficulties and students of all ages and abilities *during the first stages* of learning informative material, or material that is difficult to learn.

Rowe (2006b) refers to a very successful professional development research program (*Working Out What Works*) conducted by the Australian Council for Educational Research designed to help teachers cater more effectively for students with learning difficulties in Years 4, 5 and 6. In particular, the program encouraged teachers to use direct and explicit instruction for basic academic skills and this brought about significant improvement in students' achievements in literacy and numeracy. Improvements were also noted in students' attention to task and their general behaviour. Rowe reports that the most effective methods were found to be direct instruction, strategy training and a combination of direct instruction with strategy training. This finding confirms a large body of extant research evidence that indicates the superior effects of direct teaching over student-centred discovery methods for teaching basic skills (see Ellis, 2005 for a comprehensive review).

The use of direct teaching methods in the early stages in no way precludes students from ultimately developing independence in learning. Indeed, early direct teaching facilitates greater confidence and independence in later stages of learning. Over many decades, despite the popularity of student-centred, activity-based approaches, clear evidence supports the value of appropriate direct teaching (e.g., Kirschner et al., 2006; Mayer, 2004), often delivered through the medium of interactive whole-class lessons (Dickinson, 2003).

In general, effective teaching methods are those that provide all students with the maximum opportunity to learn by increasing 'academic engaged time' and maintaining high levels of on-task behaviour. Academic engaged time refers to the proportion of lesson time in which students are cognitively focused on their work. This active involvement includes attending to instruction from the teacher, working independently or with a group on assigned academic tasks and applying previously acquired knowledge and skills. Students who are receiving instruction directly from the teacher attend better to the content of the lesson than students who are expected to find out information for themselves. Effective lessons, particularly those covering basic academic skills, tend to have a clear structure, with effective use made of the available time. Effective teaching not only raises the attainment level of all students but also reduces significantly the prevalence of learning difficulties and disengagement (Rowe, 2006b).

Swanson (2000), after reviewing teaching methods, drew the conclusion that the most effective approach for teaching basic academic skills to students with learning difficulties combines the following features:

- carefully controlled and sequenced curriculum content
- provision of abundant opportunities for practice and application of newly acquired knowledge and skills

▶ high levels of participation and responding by the students (for example, answering the teacher's questions; staying on task)

▶ frequent feedback, correction and reinforcement from the teacher

▶ interactive group teaching

▶ modelling by the teacher of effective ways of completing school tasks

▶ teaching students how best to attempt new learning tasks (direct strategy training)

▶ appropriate use of technology (e.g. computer-assisted instruction)

▶ provision of supplementary assistance (e.g. homework, parental tutoring, etc.).

Hockenbury et al. (2000, p. 9) conclude that the education needed by students with learning difficulties includes instruction that is 'more efficient, intensive, relentless, carefully sequenced, and carefully monitored for effects'. According to Foorman et al. (2006), the features most commonly found in effective classrooms where learning difficulties are minimised include:

▶ teachers applying proactive classroom management

▶ more time devoted to instructional activities

▶ students more academically engaged

▶ more active and explicit instruction

▶ teachers providing support ('scaffolding') to help students develop deeper understanding

▶ tasks and activities well matched to students' varying abilities (differentiation)

▶ students encouraged to become more independent and self-regulated in their learning

▶ a good balance between teacher-directed and student-centred activities.

It is important to note the last point in the list above concerning *balance* between teacher-directed and student-centred learning. The work of Scruggs and Mastropieri (2007) in teaching science to students with learning problems serves to remind us that certain educational goals can't be achieved if a teacher uses *only* direct teaching methods. For example, working towards goals in science relating to inquiry and deductive reasoning clearly requires a constructive, hands-on approach, with student activity and discussion. These writers conclude that investigative activity *combined with* direct teacher input as needed is most likely to achieve the broadest range of positive outcomes in science for students with learning difficulties. In other words, the optimum approach requires a balance between teacher instruction and student construction of knowledge. A similar conclusion is warranted in relation to teaching basic academic skills in literacy and numeracy (Center, 2005; Pressley, 2006). Having reviewed the research on teaching, Ellis (2005, p. 46) concludes: 'Best practice is now recognised by classroom practitioners as the applying of a combination of instructional approaches which best fits the students being taught'.

Several researchers have used a statistical procedure known as *meta-analysis* to combine data from many different studies in order to determine the overall effectiveness of different methods of teaching or working with students with learning problems (e.g., Forness et al., 1997; Swanson, 1999; Vaughn et al., 2000). Meta-analysis allows researchers to calculate a statistic called *effect size* (ES) which can be taken as an index of the effectiveness of a particular method. An ES of 0.80 and above is regarded as a strong effect, suggesting the method produces very good results. An ES of 0.50 to 0.70 suggests a moderately effective method, while an ES below 0.30 suggests only a weak or possibly negligible effect from the method. For most purposes, it is usual to regard an effect size greater than 0.40 as indicating a potentially useful teaching approach (Cohen, 1988; Forness et al., 1997). From these meta-analyses there is strongest support for direct strategy training (e.g. teaching students to use mnemonics, apply reading comprehension strategies and strategies for writing, spelling and maths). These methods typically yield an ES above 1.0. Also strongly supported (ES of 0.70–0.85) are direct instruction and methods that involve frequent testing for mastery.

It is clear that teaching students how to learn – that is, strategy training in its various forms – combined with high-quality direct teaching of curriculum content, is most effective in helping students learn. Methods that provide abundant opportunity for practice with feedback from a teacher, high participation rates and supplementary assistance produce the best improvement (Heward, 2003). Many of the same features are identified by Sideridis and Greenwood (1998) who add the following elements to create the most effective approach for students with learning difficulties:

- reinforcement, with students being rewarded through descriptive praise and encouragement
- brisk pacing of lessons
- positive student-to-student interactions through peer assistance, group work and discussions

▶ positive student-to-teacher interactions with frequent asking and answering of questions.

Two areas of the curriculum where teaching methods exert a particularly powerful influence on students' learning are reading and mathematics. It is not the intention to go deeply into these two areas in this text because they are covered fully in other books in this series. Instead, some basic issues and principles will be considered in relation to teaching these skill-based subjects to students with learning difficulties.

Difficulties in reading

One area of the curriculum that has stimulated much attention from educational researchers over many years is the teaching of reading. Reading has also attracted major controversies regarding how it should be taught, with advocates of holistic approaches waging war against advocates for skill-based methods (Hempenstall, 2005; Santrock, 2006). The present weight of research evidence favours the view that the foundation stages of literacy and numeracy should be taught in a systematic and direct manner, rather than through a child-centred approach that relies on incidental learning (de Lemos, 2005; National Reading Panel, 2000; Rose, 2006; Wheldall & Byers, 2005). In particular, due attention should be given to the direct teaching of phonic skills to enable readers to decode unfamiliar words. It is felt that inappropriate teaching is the underlying cause of many students' difficulty in acquiring effective literacy skills.

Difficulties in acquiring proficiency in reading have also attracted much research interest. Poor reading ability is one of the major characteristics of students with learning difficulties. It is often their weakness in literacy that first brings them to the notice of teachers and parents. Ability to read is recognised as the key to effective learning in all areas of the school curriculum, so difficulty in learning to read has an extremely negative impact on a child's learning across all school subjects. Weak readers read very little, and it is an unfortunate fact that students who most need practice in order to improve through developing automaticity, fluency and confidence in their word-recognition skills are the very students who manage to engage in the least amount of reading. They use a variety of tactics to reduce the amount of time they spend engaging with books. This happens because they find reading a very frustrating and often embarrassing task. Reading difficulties thus have a detrimental influence on a student's self-esteem, confidence and motivation.

Teaching reading skills

There are two main processes involved in reading. The first is *word identification* and the second is *comprehension*. Word identification involves the accurate recognition or decoding of words printed on the page and is the first step towards reading for meaning. Many students with learning difficulties try to remember words simply by their length and pattern. While this strategy works effectively for a few words, it eventually becomes impossible to store and recall every word that is encountered. Some students with reading difficulties have not grasped that in the English language an alphabetic code is used for spelling words, and can be used in reverse to identify unfamiliar words. Using this code, letters and groups of letters represent specific speech sounds in fairly predictable ways. While it is true that some words in English are written without perfect sound-to-letter correspondences, it is equally true that at least 80 per cent of words can be decoded wholly or partly by applying phonic knowledge. So, a priority in teaching the beginning stages of reading is to establish an understanding of the phonic principle (Coltheart & Prior, 2006; de Lemos, 2004). It must be stressed here that no teacher ever uses a phonic approach *exclusively* – to do so would be to teach early reading and spelling in the most unnatural and boring way. Valid criticisms have been made of some forms of remedial teaching of reading that err on this side and involve nothing but repetitive drilling of isolated skills. The teaching of phonics needs to be done thoroughly, but only as part of a total reading program with an emphasis on reading for enjoyment and for information.

To understand the principle of phonic decoding from print, a child has to be able to break spoken words into their component sounds and know that letters can be used to represent these sounds. This concept represents one of the most essential understandings that beginning readers need to possess. Before they can understand the phonic concept they must possess what is termed *phonological awareness*. This term refers to the ability to understand that spoken words are made up from a sequence of several separate speech sounds produced in rapid succession. For example, the simple word *food* is made from the separate sounds /f/ + /oo/ + /d/. When saying the word *food* very slowly these separate sound units (*phonemes*) can be heard. Students with the most serious degrees of reading difficulty have been found to lack phonological awareness, and they need to be given structured experiences to help them improve significantly in this area (Blachman et al., 2000; Galletly, 1999; Nicholson, 2006). More information on training phonological aware-ness can be found in Westwood (2008a) within this series of books.

When children can identify sounds within spoken words the next step is to teach common letter-to-sound correspondences. Teaching phonics means teaching learners the precise relationships between letters and sounds and how sounds can be blended to produce words. The favoured method of instruction, 'synthetic phonics', is one in which children build the pronunciation of a word in print by sounding out and blending the letters. After single letter-to-sound correspondences have been mastered, instruction moves on to groups of letters that represent pronounceable parts of words (e.g. /th/,/cl/, /tr/, /str/, /pre/, /un/, /ing/, etc.), and later to the study of word families that help children recognise and use groups of letters that are shared by words that sound similar (e.g. *tell, bell, fell, cell, sell, well*).

Research evidence very strongly supports direct and systematic instruc-tion in phonic skills soon after the child reaches school age (Coltheart & Prior, 2006; Johnston & Watson, 2005). This early start provides a firm foundation on which to build higher-order literacy skills. Children should not be left to discover phonic principles for themselves through incidental learning, although much valuable phonic knowledge can be acquired and reinforced from the words children are attempting to read and write every day. There are many programs designed to teach phonic knowledge in a systematic way; for example, *THRASS* and *Jolly Phonics*, already described in Chapter 3.

As well as learning phonic skills, it is necessary for children to build up a vocabulary of words they know instantly by sight. Children who are beginners, and those with severe reading problems, do not have many words they know by sight. They have not yet had sufficient experience with reading to build up an extensive 'sight vocabulary'. But acquiring a sight vocabulary occurs quickly for most children as they gain more exposure to print. As they become competent in applying phonic knowledge to decode words, these new words are then added to a child's sight vocabulary and do not need to be decoded the next time they are met.

The key to building sight vocabulary is frequent exposure to important words and abundant practice in recognising them, saying them and writing them. Some of the usual ways of providing additional repetition and over-learning of sight vocabulary include:

▶ using vocabulary controlled reading books that deliberately use key words repetitively
▶ using flashcards to practise rapid recognition and spelling
▶ using word lotto games in which a child covers words on a card as they are pronounced by the teacher, then reads all the words back to the teacher at the end of the game.

Of course, flashcard activities and lotto games should be regarded only as *supplements* to a child's more extensive practice with reading and writing of meaningful text. Practice of sight vocabulary words and acquiring phonics skills are only of value if a child can make use of the learning when reading books and other print media. The most meaningful method of acquiring an extensive sight vocabulary is to engage in reading very frequently. Santrock (2006) summarises findings from the National Assessment of Educational Progress (NAEP) in the United States of America showing clearly that students who read more pages per day in school and for homework are much more likely to achieve higher reading test scores than those who read less. Unfortunately, students with learning difficulties are skilled in avoidance tactics and manage to read as little as possible.

Reading with understanding must be the focus of any literacy program from the very beginning. Comprehension is not something that comes *after* learning the mechanics of word recognition and decoding. Difficulties with comprehension occur if a student is weak at the underlying skill of word identification. Slow and laboured reading prevents easy interpretation of meaning. Students who are good at comprehending text use a variety of ways to support their understanding. For example, they may visualise as they read narrative material; they may pose questions to themselves; they may think about the relevance of what they are reading; they may challenge the accuracy of stated facts; and they check their own understanding as they read. Weaker readers do not tend to use any of these strategies spontaneously.

In order to improve students' comprehension, it is important to consider the possible underlying cause of the problem. Sometimes comprehension problems stem from a student's limited vocabulary knowledge or lack of reading fluency. If a student has difficulty understanding what is read, it is worth devoting more time to discussing word meanings, before, during and after the student reads a passage of text. There is certainly value in sometimes pre-teaching difficult vocabulary. Engaging readers in discussion about the topic of a text and encouraging them to adopt a thoughtful approach can also improve their reading comprehension most naturally. It is also necessary to teach students effective strategies to use when approaching text in order to get meaning from it (Boulware-Gooden et al., 2007). Such strategies include:

- previewing the text first to get an overall impression of the content
- generating questions in your mind concerning what you already know about the topic and what you hope to find out
- reading the text carefully, and then rereading if necessary
- summarising in your mind the main points in what you have read.

Unfortunately, there is evidence that primary school teachers tend not to give sufficient attention to strategy instruction in reading (Parker & Hurry, 2007). And in secondary schools comprehension tends to be tested, rather than taught.

The following principles may also help to strengthen comprehension skill development for students with learning difficulties:

- Ensure that the reading material is interesting and at an appropriate reading level.
- Always make sure students are aware of the purpose for reading a particular text.
- Apply comprehension strategy training, using authentic texts rather than contrived exercises.
- Prepare students for starting a new book. Ask: 'What do you think this story is about?' 'What do the illustrations tell us?' 'What does this word mean?' 'Let's read the subheadings before we begin'.
- If there are comprehension questions to be answered, read them together *before* the story or passage is read, so that students enter the material knowing what information to seek.
- Use newspapers and magazine articles as the basis for discussion and comprehension activities. Highlighter pens can be used to focus upon key ideas, important terms, or facts to remember.

Key elements in fostering reading development

It has already been stressed that daily instruction will achieve much more than twice-weekly intervention, and that maximum progress occurs when parents or others can provide additional support and practice beyond school hours. In addition, to prevent or remedy difficulties in reading, teachers should ensure that the following elements are provided within the teaching program:

▶ abundant opportunities to read for pleasure and for information

▶ systematic instruction in phonic knowledge and word-attack skills

▶ opportunities to build a sight vocabulary of the most frequently used words

▶ successful practice, often using material that has become familiar to the student

▶ practice that will build skills to a high level of automaticity and at the same time strengthen a student's confidence

▶ texts used with students must be carefully selected to ensure a very high success rate

▶ instruction and guided practice in applying reading comprehension strategies

▶ counselling, praise, encouragement and recognition of personal progress in order to improve a student's self-esteem

▶ as well as attempting to improve reading, teachers must also focus on the correction of any negative behaviours such as poor attention to task and task avoidance that are impairing a student's progress.

Difficulties in learning mathematics

Many students, including those without learning difficulties, find mathematics a difficult subject to master; and many go through life regarding themselves as poor mathematicians. Some even develop a phobia and learned helplessness regarding mathematics, and they panic at the thought of having to perform calculations and solve problems (Buxton, 1991). Wain (1994) considers it a very sad commentary on mathematics teaching that it has failed so many students by not providing them with stimulation, understanding, enjoyment and a feeling of success. He points out that many intelligent people, after an average of 1500 hours of instruction over eleven years of schooling still regard mathematics as a subject for which they have no aptitude. Their antipathy toward the subject continues into adult life.

Yet, there is no convincing evidence (with a few exceptions) that their difficulties are the result of any perceptual or cognitive deficits. The few exceptions are the students with a genuine learning disability ('dyscalculia'), perhaps affecting up to 3 per cent of the population (Colwell, 2003; Michaelson, 2007). According to Landerl et al. (2004), dyscalculia is due to a brain-based deficit that specifically affects numerical processing, and is not due to weaknesses in other cognitive processes such as attention, memory or perception. Given that some 35–40 per cent of students are reported to have difficulties with mathematics (American Institutes for Research, 2006), it is clear that dyscalculia explains only a tiny part of this population. For the remaining individuals, it is likely that the curriculum content and the teaching methods used are the cause of failure to learn.

Some of the negative pedagogical factors associated with learning difficulties in mathematics include:

▶ insufficient or inappropriate instruction
▶ curriculum covered too rapidly, outstripping students' ability to learn
▶ lack of balance between direct instruction in basic computational processes and student-centred activity
▶ abstract concepts and symbols introduced in the absence of real-life concrete examples
▶ poorly structured or overly complex textbook.

Regardless of the innate and environmental causes of failure in mathematics, students with difficulties all tend to show the following weaknesses:

▶ poor mathematical concept development
▶ lack of understanding of mathematical terms
▶ confusion over the meaning of printed symbols and signs
▶ extremely poor recall of basic number facts
▶ weak multiplication skills
▶ difficulty in understanding place-value (e.g. that in the number 2072 the first numeral on the left represents 2000 while the final numeral represents 2 units)
▶ poor procedural skills leading to slowness and frustration in calculating
▶ inability to determine which processes to use in solving problems
▶ untidy bookwork with misaligned columns of figures
▶ frequent reversal of single figures and reversal of tens and units (e.g. 34 written as 43)

▶ difficulties with reading and comprehending word problems

▶ lack of effective strategies for approaching mathematical tasks

▶ inability to transfer mathematical skills taught in school to the real world.

Teaching basic mathematics

The most effective teachers of mathematics appear to provide systematic instruction in a way that students not only master arithmetic skills and problem-solving strategies but also develop a genuine understanding of the subject matter (Hay et al., 2005). Research on teacher effectiveness in the area of mathematics, together with some influential views on mathematics teaching, support the use of a structured approach within a carefully sequenced program rather than purely activity-based methods (DfCSF, 2007; Ellis, 2005; Kilpatrick et al., 2001; Stigler & Hiebert, 2004). Emphasis is placed upon students constructing meaning rather than memorising facts and procedures through rote learning; but this is not achieved simply through the medium of unstructured activities. Effective lessons are typically clear, accurate and rich in examples of a particular concept, process, or strategy, with ample opportunities for students to practise and apply what they have learned. The emerging perspective is that effective teaching and learning in mathematics for all students requires not only student-centred investigative activities but also a good measure of teacher-directed explicit instruction.

It is essential to help students with learning difficulties develop functional arithmetic skills and effective problem-solving strategies. Functional knowledge in arithmetic involves two major components:

▶ mastery of basic number facts that can be automatically retrieved rapidly from memory (e.g. 9×4)

▶ a body of knowledge about computational procedures for subtraction, addition, multiplication and division.

The National Council of Teachers of Mathematics (NCTM) (2000) in the United States of America affirms that all students should develop fluency in operations with numbers, using swift mental computation and paper-and-pencil calculations. This ability is also stressed in the activities recommended for the daily 'numeracy hour' in UK primary schools. However, it is vital that teachers recognise that skill in arithmetic is a necessary *but insufficient* component of competence in functional mathematics. On top of this competency, students also need effective cognitive strategies to apply when faced with mathematical problems.

When focusing on remediation with students with learning difficulties it is advisable to use a diagnostic approach, starting with finding out what they can already do, and what concepts and skills they have already acquired (Hay et al., 2005). It is also essential to locate any gaps in knowledge that may exist (for example, weakness in certain multiplication facts, or misconceptions regarding a particular process) and to determine what the student needs to be taught next. This information can be obtained by looking at samples of a student's work, setting suitably graded tests and analysing the results, and from working directly with the student in an informal interview situation. Where a student is experiencing difficulty with particular types of calculation, it is revealing to discover whether the student can carry out the process if allowed to use counters, a number line, or a calculator. Can the student explain and demonstrate what to do to perform a particular calculation or solve a specific problem? The student can be asked to work through the example step by step, thinking aloud throughout the process. The teacher can then detect at once the exact point of difficulty or confusion and can intervene from there.

Students with learning difficulties usually display helplessness and confusion when faced with mathematical problems in word form. They may, for example, have difficulty reading the problem and comprehending the exact meaning of specific terms. They do not know how or where to begin, or what process to use. Their most obvious weakness is a lack of any effective plan of action for approaching a mathematical task. Students with these difficulties need to be taught a range of effective problem-solving and task-approach strategies. The aim is to teach them how to process information in a word problem without a feeling of panic or hopelessness. They need to be able to sift information sensibly and impose some degree of structure for solving the problem.

While current wisdom on the teaching of mathematics favours a problem-based approach, students with learning difficulties tend to get lost, and they learn very little if left to discover methods of calculation and problem solving incidentally. They need to be taught directly and sequentially the knowledge and skills required in functional mathematics. When teaching a problem-solving strategy the teacher should:

- model and demonstrate effective use of the strategy for solving routine and non-routine problems
- 'think aloud' as each aspect of the problem is analysed
- discuss with the students possible procedures for calculating a result
- reflect upon the effectiveness of the procedure and the feasibility of the result obtained.

Once students have been taught a particular strategy they need an opportunity to apply the strategy under teacher guidance and with feedback. Finally, they must be able to use the strategy independently and generalise its use to other problems. The sequence for instruction in problem solving of students with learning difficulties therefore follows a logical sequence beginning with direct teaching, followed by guided practice and ending with student-centred control and independence. It is clear that for students with learning difficulties it is necessary to provide many more examples than usual to establish and strengthen the application of a particular strategy. Since there is evidence that students can be helped to become more proficient at solving problems, teachers of students with learning difficulties need to devote adequate time to this important area of schoolwork and not confine their teaching to pure arithmetic. Appropriate balance within the program is the key.

LINKS TO MORE ON TEACHING METHODS

- The books *Teaching and learning difficulties* (Westwood, 2006) and *What teachers need to know about teaching methods* (Westwood, 2008b) address in much more detail many of the issues raised in this chapter.
- The Center for Literacy Studies at the University of Tennessee provides a helpful summary of the most effective teaching methods for students (including adults) with learning difficulties. Available online at: http://ldlink.coe.utk.edu/characteristics_of_ld.htm
- The National Center for Learning Disabilities (US) provides information on classroom strategies for grades K to 8. Available online at: http://www.ncld.org/content/view/304/376/

>

- The National Dissemination Centre for Children with Disabilities website has helpful material on strategy training (*News Digest 25*). Available online at: http://www.nichcy.org/pubs/newsdig/nd25txt.htm
- The Reading Reform Foundation website contains many valuable items on the effective teaching of literacy skills. The material is constantly updated. Available online at: http://www.rrf.org.uk/
- *LDonline* website has a paper by Kate Garnett on 'math learning disability'. Available online at: http://www.ldonline.org/article/5896
- Details of the *Reading Assistance Kit*, developed as a component of the Reading Assistance Voucher Scheme in Australia (2007) are available online at: http://www.readingtuition.edu.au

Accommodating and supporting students with learning difficulties

▶ Students with learning difficulties can have their instructional needs met in a variety of ways; for example by adapting the curriculum, modifying the teaching method, varying the teaching materials, or through supplementary instruction.

▶ Most of these strategies for accommodating students with learning difficulties bring with them some disadvantages or limitations as well as benefits.

▶ One common characteristic of all effective support strategies is that they increase the student's academic engaged time, provide additional successful practice and increase a student's self-efficacy and confidence.

Students with learning difficulties require various forms of support in order to learn more effectively and, if possible, catch up with their peer group in terms of academic achievement and social development. This support can come in many different forms, ranging from modifications to the classroom program, an individual education plan, changes to the pattern of organisation within the classroom, providing additional teaching either within the class or by withdrawal for group instruction, peer tutoring, using additional support staff to give the student individual help, or any feasible combination of these options. Support may also be provided through access to additional specialist services and resources beyond those available in the school (e.g. for psychological assessment, speech therapy, counselling) (Dettmer et al., 2005). In this final chapter some of the in-school systems of support will be discussed.

Adapting the classroom program

Fletcher-Campbell et al. (1999, p. 73) state categorically that, 'Education has to adapt to pupils', implying that a one-size-fits-all approach to teaching is untenable if students' individual needs are to be met. The term *differentiation* – meaning teaching things differently according to observed differences among students – has been used to describe the practice of attempting to match instruction to students' characteristics. Adapting instruction in this way is essential for students with significant disabilities. But differentiation obviously has potential benefits too for students with learning difficulties if it means that schoolwork can be tailored to meet their needs. According to van den Berg et al. (2001, p. 246):

> Adaptive teaching is an educational approach that clearly recognises differences between learners – especially cognitive differences or other specific characteristics. Teachers accept that their students differ in capabilities and *take these differences as the starting point for teaching and learning.* [emphasis added]

Differentiation can occur in terms of adjustments to the curriculum content, the teaching-learning processes and the products from each lesson. Differentiation can also occur through modification of the instructional materials, the classroom organisation, student–teacher interactions, the amount of support given to different students, modifications to the nature of assigned homework and accommodations made in methods of assessment (Fahsl, 2007; Janney & Snell, 2004; Tomlinson, 1996, 2001). Effective differentiation combines pedagogical and organisational adjustments. Differentiation is also achieved through flexible use of support staff, changing the learning environment, setting alternative tasks, using assistive technology and providing variety in the ways students are required to produce work. Each of these forms of differentiation can bring both benefits and disadvantages, as indicated here.

Adapting curriculum content

This usually means that students with learning difficulties may be required to cover less material in a lesson (or deal with the content in less depth) and the resource materials such as texts, worksheets and notes may be modified to require less reading and writing. Homework may contain activities for additional practice and application rather than extension work. While this form of modification makes it easier for students to succeed, they may actually dislike it intensely because it clearly highlights them as less capable than other students, and is thus embarrassing within the peer group (Hall, 1997; Klinger & Vaughn, 1999). On this issue Seligman (1995) says that if we deprive students of the opportunity to work towards the same objectives as other students we weaken their self-esteem just as certainly as if we had overtly belittled or humiliated them. Shaddock (2006) recommends that teachers should avoid offering a diluted and self-limiting curriculum. Reducing or 'watering down' content also has the long-term effect of increasing the learning gap between students with learning difficulties and other students. Wang (1998) has reported there is evidence that students may receive less high-quality instruction when schools try to modify the work and individualise the curriculum in this way.

Adapting teaching and learning processes

This adaptation covers all the major and minor changes that may be made to the way instruction occurs in the classroom. It includes modifications to the teaching method, how students are grouped, the nature of their participation in the lesson and interactions between teacher and students. The teacher may re-teach certain concepts or information to some students, perhaps using simpler language and more examples. A teacher may give more assistance or less assistance to individuals according to their needs. Questions asked during the lesson may be pitched at different levels of difficulty to increase participation, and there may be closer monitoring of the work of some students during the lesson. The rate at which the students are expected to work is allowed to vary, with extra time allowed for some, and extra practice provided for those who need it. Cooperative learning, peer assistance and group work may be used to ensure that students with difficulties can benefit from working successfully with others. For some areas of the curriculum, computer-assisted instruction (CAI) may be used. The advantage of this form of differentiation for students with learning difficulties is that the modifications can be applied while still following a common curriculum with the class. For this reason, they are regarded as the easiest adaptations for teachers to make. Deschenes et al. (1999, p. 13) observe that, 'Adapting in this way is feasible for classroom teachers because it is relatively unobtrusive, requiring little extra time for special planning'. From the students' point of view, it is less likely that the gap will expand between higher and lower achievers.

Adapting outcomes and products

Outcomes from the learning process are often tangible products such as written work, graphics, or a model; but sometimes the product refers to other evidence of learning, such as an oral report, a performance, a presentation to the group, participation in discussion, or the answering of oral questions. The outcomes or products provide one form of evidence that learning has occurred. Modifying the products of learning may mean that each student is not expected to produce exactly the same amount, type, or quality of work as every other student. A student may be asked to produce work in a different format, for example, an audio recording, a drawing or poster, rather than an essay. Or a student may complete a multiple-choice exercise rather than prepare an assignment involving extensive writing. A potential danger in setting out from the start to accept less work from some students, or a lower quality of work, is that this strategy represents a lowering of expectations that can result in a self-fulfilling prophecy. A different perspective suggests that teachers should help students with learning difficulties achieve more, not less, in terms of output. Removing all obstacles may not be in the best interest of these students.

Differentiation of assessment

Assessment refers to any process used to determine how much learning and what quality of learning has occurred for each student in the class. Assessment provides an indication of how effective a particular episode of teaching and learning has been. Assessment also highlights anything that may need to be taught again, revised, or practised more by some students.

Classroom tests are one of the ways in which teachers assess the progress of their students. Students with significant learning difficulties may require additional time to complete the test, or a variation in the mode of responding. Students who have a genuine learning disability such as dyslexia can, in some countries, obtain permission to take public examinations with the help of a scribe or interpreter, or with more time allowed.

Obviously, modifications or accommodations to assessment should not result in the abilities of students with a learning difficulty being misrepresented as greater than they really are in school reports. The intention is to help the students reveal accurately what they know, without having to place emphasis on written responses and reading. Modifications to assessment for students with learning difficulties include such options as:

▶ simplifying or abbreviating the assessment task
▶ allowing longer time for some students to complete the task or test
▶ allowing students with literacy problems to have assistance in performing the task or test (e.g. having the questions read to them, or dictating answers to a scribe)
▶ allowing a student to present work in a different format (e.g. a project book or portfolio, rather than an essay).

Difficulties with differentiation

Although differentiation is widely recommended in policy documents and teaching guidelines, adjusting instruction and modifying the approach in this way is far from easy. Many teachers are unable or reluctant to engage in extensive changes to the way they commonly teach a group of students because it requires a large amount of additional planning every day and is difficult to sustain over time (Chan et al., 2002; Fuchs & Fuchs, 1998). Studies have found that teachers have major problems when attempting to match the difficulty level of classroom tasks to the different cognitive ability levels of their students. In the American context, Schumm and Vaughn (1995, p. 176) observe, 'Despite a growing body of literature regarding instructional adaptations that teachers can make in general education settings, few teachers implement such accommodations'. With this in mind, rather than using complicated systems of differentiated teaching, students with learning difficulties may be better served by greatly improving the quality of general classroom teaching and providing additional support for those who are still in need. This is entirely compatible with the notion of 'tiers' or 'waves' of intervention, as described in Chapter 3.

Individual Education Plan

An Individual Education Plan (IEP) is a document drawn up by relevant personnel (teacher, psychologist, speech therapist, parents, etc.) to indicate clearly the learning objectives and required methods of instruction for a student with special educational needs. In most schools, students with *general* learning difficulties are unlikely to have an IEP; but students ascertained as having SpLD may have such a document. The advantage of having an IEP is that teachers have a clear indication of what to aim for with the student, and progress is monitored regularly. An IEP often indicates that the student is entitled to a certain amount of additional time with a support teacher or teacher's aide for individual teaching. An IEP can result in more effective support being available to a student with learning difficulties. Tennant (2007) suggests that the process of creating an IEP is valuable in itself by getting staff to spend time thinking of the priority needs of particular students and how best to meet those needs.

Organising support in school

There are four main ways in which support and additional teaching are provided for students with learning difficulties in primary and secondary schools:

- *in-class support:* additional help is provided by the classroom teacher, resource teacher, teacher's aide, volunteer helper, or through peer-tutoring
- *resource room model:* at designated times, students with learning difficulties leave the mainstream class to attend sessions with the special education teacher in the resource room
- *special class:* students are placed full-time or part-time in a class containing other students with learning problems to follow an intensive remedial program
- *ability grouping:* a pattern of school organisation that groups students into classes based on academic ability (also referred to as *streaming* or *tracking*).

In-class support became the favoured model in the past decade, because it was believed that students felt stigmatised by being withdrawn from class to attend resource room teaching. The in-class support model is also in keeping with the philosophy of inclusive schooling that suggests all children have the right to be in mainstream classes, and that all teachers should accommodate the full ability range without handing some students over to other staff for different treatment elsewhere. By providing support within the student's own class, it is believed that help can be given within the context of the mainstream curriculum, not via a separate program. The big disadvantage of in-class support is that it draws immediate and obvious attention to the students receiving the help. For this reason, it is not always popular, particularly with secondary school students.

The resource room model can be quite effective if the students attend the sessions willingly. The smaller group context makes it feasible to address individual needs and differences. It is also easier for the teacher to adopt a direct instruction approach that research has shown to be highly effective (Carnine, 2000). Primary school students tend to prefer attending resource room lessons rather than receiving in-class support (Vlachou et al., 2006), but students in secondary school prefer to remain in class without additional assistance other than that provided by the teacher in the normal course of the lesson. In some schools the staff in a resource room also provide a service to other teachers by creating alternative instructional materials for use in the mainstream (e.g. simplified texts, worksheets, computer software).

Full-time and part-time special classes were popular before the advent of inclusive education practices. They had many of the advantages of a resource room in terms of the opportunity to structure the program tightly and use effective instructional methods. The great disadvantage was that they segregated the students from the mainstream, and the students often hated being stigmatised as 'special'. Although many of these classes were called 'opportunity classes' they actually reduced a student's opportunity to return to the mainstream because the curriculum content tended to differ in the two settings. There is abundant evidence that being placed in a special class can have lasting negative effects on the students' motivation, self-esteem and feelings of self-efficacy (e.g., Alderman, 1999; Cross & Vidyarthi, 2000).

Ability grouping or streaming was once very popular, and although less popular now, it is still retained in many secondary schools. It is argued that grouping students by academic ability creates homogeneous classes that are easier to teach, particularly in key subjects such as mathematics, science and foreign languages (Hallam, 1996; Oakes, 1994). Students with learning difficulties would be accommodated in lower streams, along with other students who were displaying poor achievement. In theory, ability grouping should facilitate the broad differentiation of curriculum content into at least three levels (advanced, standard and basic). Such adjustments, it is argued, can result in enhanced opportunities to experience success rather than failure. It is sometimes suggested that students with learning difficulties can be helped most by ability-grouping practices because they no longer have to compete with, or compare themselves to, the most capable students (Harlen & Malcolm, 1997). Students of high ability are also believed to benefit from ability-grouping practices because they can be exposed to a suitably challenging program. Ability grouping became less popular, however, for a variety of reasons, not least because it did not appear to deliver most of the expected benefits. In particular, research results have suggested that grouping by ability does nothing to raise the achievement level of the lower-ability students. There are also potential problems associated with placing students with learning difficulties permanently in what are perceived as 'bottom' groups – such as negative social labelling effects, reduced curriculum coverage, removal of opportunities for lower-achieving students to work with and learn from high-achieving students, and a widening of the gap between high-ability and low-ability classes in terms of achievement. Students in low-track classes typically have the most negative views of themselves both academically and generally (Oakes, 1985). In recent years, the trend has therefore been toward mixed-ability classes in both primary and secondary schools. Mixed-ability classes, it is believed, offer an equal opportunity for all students to participate in a common curriculum. Within mixed-ability settings, effective in-class support and curriculum differentiation can be offered as necessary. However, Good and Brophy (2008) have commented that abolition of ability grouping, while strongly advocated by many educators, is not unanimously supported. They regard arguments for mixed-ability teaching as based more on ideological, sociological and theoretical principles than on any empirical evidence demonstrating its effectiveness.

Most schools appear to adopt some combination of the four models described above. Each model has some advantages and some definite dis-advantages. Schools adopt particular models partly based on the school's philosophy concerning how best to support students with learning difficulties, but partly on the availability of necessary human and material resources.

Additional teaching

One of the ways in which students with learning difficulties are supported is through additional teaching, either within the class or through part-time withdrawal for group or individual instruction. Many countries now employ 'support teachers' or 'resource teachers', and may also supplement the effort of these teachers by using paraprofessionals – variously known as 'classroom assistants', 'learning support assistants', 'or 'teacher's aides'. These additional personnel, together with a growing number of volunteer helpers in schools, are regarded as integral and essential components of an effective support system for students integrated into inclusive classrooms (Fox, 2003). In recent years, resource teachers have been encouraged to widen the scope of their remedial help so that they work more in support of other teachers in the school and less in direct teaching of students with learning difficulties in a withdrawal room.

Co-teaching and in-class support are increasingly presented as desirable models of service delivery; but students requiring 'third-wave' intensive teaching are still likely to benefit most from separate sessions, at least in the early stages. Some research indicates that a combination of in-class support together with regular withdrawal for intensive instruction produces the best gains in achievement (Marston, 1996).

As indicated above, in-class support can be provided by the students' own teacher, by a support teacher, or by a teacher's aide working under the direction of the teacher. In the past decade the value of paraprofessionals assisting within the classroom has been recognised in most education systems (Department for Education and Skills, UK, 2004; Dettmer et al., 2005). While paraprofessionals are not responsible for determining the details of the curriculum content to be followed by a student with learning difficulties, or for setting the objectives and selecting methods, they can be instrumental in helping the student access the curriculum and achieve the objectives. A classroom assistant can contribute to the teaching and learning by working closely with individual students, working with small groups, helping to interpret instructions, checking for understanding, keeping students on task, listening to students read, modifying tasks or materials, supervising and giving feedback on practice activities, and generally encouraging and motivating students (Logan, 2006). Classroom assistants have an important role in pastoral care. They can be invaluable as an extra 'ear' for detecting students' worries and disputes.

In many parts of Australia, schools have created what are often called 'Learning Assistance Programs' (LAPs) using parents, grandparents, retired teachers, student-teachers, or other unpaid workers to help students with learning problems – and sometimes to work with gifted and talented students as part of a 'mentor' scheme. These volunteers perform a very valuable service in schools. When assisting students with learning problems the roles given to such helpers include listening to individual students read (providing extra practice), helping students with writing and spelling, helping students check or prepare homework assignments, and sitting with a student to keep him or her on task. The amount of individual attention they can devote to students with special needs is far greater than most teachers can afford to give.

Peer tutoring is another option that can provide additional support for learning. In peer tutoring situations one student instructs or rehearses another student on a prescribed topic. The tutoring process results in much greater individual attention for the tutee, and also has benefits for the tutor. Students are often much more effective communicators than are teachers when it comes to explaining a concept or demonstrating a skill. In most classrooms where peer tutoring, cross-age tutoring (older students working with younger students) or class-wide peer tutoring (all students involved) are implemented have discovered that tutors need some amount of training in order to carry out their role effectively. They need training in providing positive feedback, using praise, explaining, elaborating, rehearsing and reinforcement. It is also important to match tutor with tutee carefully to ensure compatibility. The evidence is that peer tutoring can be very effective in achieving both social and academic gains (Cole & Chan, 1990; McMaster et al., 2006).

There are, of course, several other ways in which students with learning difficulties can have additional teaching, adapted to their ability and needs. For example, computer-assisted learning has much to offer in terms of drill and practice programs and instructional packages, after-hours tutoring at school and private tutoring arranged by parents outside school hours.

It can be seen from the above descriptions that there are many options open to teachers to help accommodate and support students with learning difficulties more effectively. Chan and Dally (2001b, p. 18) conclude that there is no single model that is able to meet the diverse needs of all students; and that '… students with learning difficulties are best served by having access to a range of services that can operate simultaneously and flexibly'. It is to be hoped that all schools seek to provide such services and such flexibility.

LINKS TO MORE ON SUPPORT FOR LEARNING

▶ The TeacherNet website provides an overview of Learning Support Units in the UK. Available online at: http://www.teachernet.gov.uk/wholeschool/behaviour/learningsupportunits/

▶ New Zealand Ministry of Education website outlines the Supplementary Learning Support system operating in that country. Available online at: http://www.minedu.govt.nz/goto/SLS

▶ Support systems in NSW public schools are described online at: http://www.schools.nsw.edu.au/studentsupport/programs/lrngdifficulty.php

▶ Similar information on support in South Australia is available at: http://decs.sa.gov.au/speced/pages/speced/learning_difficulties/?showback=1

▶ In-class support strategies are described at: http://www.simonmidgley.co.uk/support/inclass.htm

▶ Information on peer tutoring and cross-age tutoring is available online at: http://www.nwrel.org/scpd/sirs/9/c018.htm and at: www.indiana.edu/~reading/ieo/digests/d78.html

▶ Information on ability grouping and the evidence from research is available online at: http://www.sharingsuccess.org/code/bv/abilitygrouping.pdf

References

Abosi, O. (2007). Educating children with learning disabilities in Africa. *Learning Disabilities Research and Practice, 22, 3*, 196–201.

Alderman, M. K. (1999). *Motivation for achievement: Possibilities for teaching and learning.* Mahwah, NJ: Erlbaum.

Allen, D., James, W., Evans, J., Hawkins, S., & Jenkins, R. (2005). Positive behavioural support: Definition, current status and future directions. *Tizard Learning Disability Review, 10, 2*, 4–1.

Altarac, M., & Saroha, E. (2007). Lifetime prevalence of learning disability among US children. *Pediatrics, 119 (supplement)*, S77–S83.

American Institutes for Research. (2006). *A review of the literature on adult numeracy: Research and conceptual issues.* Washington, DC: American Institutes for Research.

APA (American Psychiatric Association). (2000). *Diagnostic and statistical manual of mental disorders: Text revised (DSM–IV–TR).* Washington, DC: APA.

Arkansas Department of Education (Special Education). (2007). *Resource guide for specific learning disabilities.* Retrieved January 20, 2008 from: http://arksped.k12.ar.us/documents/stateprogramdevelopment/DyslexiaGuideApril30.pdf

Atkinson, J. W. (1966). Motivational determinants of risk taking behavior. In J. W. Atkinson & N. T. Feather (Eds.), *A theory of achievement motivation* (pp. 11–31). New York: Wiley.

Badian, N. A. (1996). Dyslexia: A validation of the concept at two age levels. *Journal of Learning Disabilities, 29, 1*, 102–112.

Bakker, J. T. A., & Bosman, A. M. T. (2006). Teachers' perceptions of remediation possibilities of Dutch students in special education. *British Journal of Educational Psychology, 76*, 745–759.

Barrett, W., & Randall, L. (2004). Investigating the Circle of Friends approach: Adaptations and implications for practice. *Educational Psychology in Practice, 20, 4*, 353–68.

Barton-Arwood, S., Morrow, L., Lane, K., & Jolivette, K. (2005). Project IMPROVE: Improving teachers' ability to address students' social needs. *Education and Treatment of Children, 28, 4*, 430–443.

Bender, W. N. (2004). *Learning disabilities: Characteristics, identification, and teaching strategies.* (5th ed.). Boston: Allyn & Bacon.

Biggs, J. (1995). Motivating learning. In J. Biggs, & D. Watkins (Eds.), *Classroom learning* (pp. 82–102). Singapore: Prentice Hall.

Blachman, B. A., Ball, E. W., Black, R., & Tangel, D. M. (2000). *Road to the Code: A phonological awareness program for young children.* Baltimore, MD: Brookes.

Boekaerts, M. (1996). Social, cultural and affective aspects of learning. In E. de Corte, & F. E. Weinert (Eds.), *International encyclopedia of developmental and instructional psychology* (pp. 585–590). Oxford: Pergamon.

Boulware-Gooden, R., Carreker, S., Thornhill, A., & Joshi, R. M. (2007). Instruction in metacognitive strategies enhances reading comprehension and vocabulary achievement of Third-Grade students. *Reading Teacher, 61, 1,* 7–77.

Bradley, R., Danielson, L., & Hallahan, D. P. (Eds.), (2002). *Identification of learning disabilities: Research and practice.* Mahwah, NJ: Erlbaum.

Brooks, G. (2002). *What works for children with literacy difficulties? The effectiveness of intervention schemes. Research Report 380.* London: Department for Education and Skills. Retrieved January 28, 2008 from: http://www.dfes.gov.uk/research/data/uploadfiles/RR380.pdf

Brophy, J. (1998). Failure syndrome students. *ERIC Digest: EDO-PS-98-2.* Retrieved January 26, 2008 from: http://ceep.crc.uiuc.edu/eecearchive/digests/1998/brophy98.pdf

Bryan, T. (1998). Social competence of students with learning disabilities. In B. Y. L. Wong (Ed.), *Learning about learning disabilities* (2nd ed., pp. 237–267). San Diego, CA: Academic Press.

Bryan, T. (2003). The applicability of the risk and resilience model to social problems of students with learning disabilities: Response to Bernice Wong. *Learning Disabilities Research and Practice, 18, 2,* 94–98.

Bryer, F., Beamish, W., Davies, M., Marshall, R., Wilson, L., & Caldwell, W. (2005). The first steps to school-wide positive behavioural support in a Queensland high school: Laying the foundation for participation. *Special Education Perspectives, 14, 2,* 26–45.

Burden, B. (2002). A cognitive approach to dyslexia: learning styles and thinking skills. In G. Reid & J. Wearmouth (Eds.), *Dyslexia and literacy* (pp. 271–283). Chichester: Wiley.

Buxton, L. (1991). *Math panic.* Portsmouth, NH: Heinemann.

Cadman, A. (1976). *Learning difficulties in children and adults: Report of the House of Representatives Select Committee on Specific Learning Difficulties.* Canberra: Australian Government Publishing Service.

Campbell, F. A., & Ramey, C. T. (1994). Effects of early intervention on intellectual and academic achievement. *Child Development, 65, 2,* 684–698.

Carlson, S. (2005). *A two hundred year history of learning disabilities*. ERIC document. Retrieved January 12, 2008 from: eric.ed.gov/ERICDocs/data/ericdocs2sql/content_storage_01/0000019b/80/1b/c3/e4.pdf

Carnine, D. (2000). *Why education experts resist effective practices (and what it would take to make education more like medicine)*. Washington, DC: Thomas B. Fordham Foundation.

Cartledge, G. (2005). Learning disabilities and social skills: Reflections. *Learning Disability Quarterly, 28, 2*, 179–81.

Center, Y. (2005). *Beginning reading: A balanced approach to literacy during the first three years at school*. Sydney: Allen & Unwin.

Center, Y., Freeman, L., & Robertson, G. (1998). An evaluation of the Schoolwide Early Literacy and Language Program (SWELL) in six disadvantaged NSW schools. *International Journal of Disability, Development and Education, 45*, 143–172.

Chalk, J. C., Hagan-Burke, S., & Burke, M. D. (2005). The effects of self-regulated strategy development on the writing process for high school students with learning disabilities. *Learning Disability Quarterly, 28, 1*, 75–87.

Chan, C., Chang, M. L., Westwood, P., & Yuen, M. T. (2002). Teaching adaptively: How easy is 'differentiation' in practice? A perspective from Hong Kong. *Asia-Pacific Educational Researcher 11, 1*, 27–58.

Chan, L. K. S. (1994). Relationship of motivation, strategic learning and reading achievement in Grades 5, 7 and 9. *Journal of Experimental Education, 62, 4*, 319–339.

Chan, L. K. S., & Dally, K. (2000). Review of literature. In W. Louden, L. Chan, J. Elkins, D. Greaves, H. House, M. Milton, S. Nichols, M. Rohl, J. Rivalland, & C. van Kraayenoord (Eds.), *Mapping the territory: Primary students with learning difficulties in literacy and numeracy*. Canberra: Department of Education, Training and Youth Affairs.

Chan, L. K. S., & Dally, K. (2001a). Learning disabilities and literacy and numeracy development. *Australian Journal of Learning Disabilities, 6, 1*, 12–19.

Chan, L. K. S., & Dally, K. (2001b). Instructional techniques and service delivery approaches for students with learning difficulties. *Australian Journal of Learning Disabilities, 6, 3*, 14–21.

Chan, L. K. S., & van Kraayenoord, C. E. (1998). Learning through dialogues for students with learning difficulties. *Australian Journal of Learning Disabilities, 3, 1*, 21–26.

Chang, C. C., & Westwood, P. (2001). The effects of ability grouping on low-achievers' motivation and teachers' expectations. *Hong Kong Special Education Forum, 4, 1*, 27–48.

Charles, C. M., & Senter, G. W. (2005). *Elementary classroom management* (4th ed.). Boston: Pearson-Allyn & Bacon.

Clay, M. M. (1993). *Reading Recovery: A guidebook for teachers in training.* Auckland: Heinemann.

Clerehugh, J., Hart, K., Pither, R., Rider, K., & Turner, K. (1991). *Early Years Easy Screen* (EYES). London: NFER-Nelson.

Cohen, J. (1988). *Statistical power analysis for the behavioral sciences* (2nd ed.). New York: Academic Press.

Cole, P., & Chan, L .K. S. (1990). *Methods and strategies for special education.* Sydney: Prentice Hall.

Coleman, P. K., & Byrd, C. P. (2000). Interpersonal correlates of peer victimization among young adolescents. *Journal of Youth and Adolescence, 32, 4,* 301–314.

Coltheart, M., & Prior, M. (2006). Learning to read in Australia. *Australian Journal of Learning Disabilities, 11, 4,* 157–164.

Colwell, D. (2003). Dyscalculia and functioning of the brain in mathematical activity. In D. Coben (Ed.), *Adult numeracy: review of research and related literature* (pp. 104–109). London: National Research and Development Centre for Adult Literacy and Numeracy.

Crevola, C. A., & Hill, P. W. (1998). Evaluation of a whole-school approach to prevention and intervention in early literacy. *Journal of Education for Students Placed at Risk, 3, 2,* 133–157.

Cross, M., & Vidyarthi, A. (2000). Permission to fail. *Special Children, 126,* 13–15.

Davies, A., & Ritchie, D. (2004). *Teaching Handwriting, Reading and Spelling Skills (THRASS).* Chester: THRASS (UK) Ltd.

de Lemos, M. M. (2004). Effective strategies for the teaching of reading: What works, and why. In B. A. Knight & W. Scott (Eds.), *Learning difficulties: Multiple perspectives* (pp. 17–28). Frenchs Forest, NSW: Pearson Educational.

de Lemos, M. M. (2005). Effective strategies for the teaching of reading: What works and why. *Australian Journal of Learning Disabilities, 10, 3/4,* 11–17.

Delgado, C. E. F., Vagi, S. J., & Scott, K. G. (2007). Identification of early risk factors for developmental delay. *Exceptionality, 15, 2,* 119–136.

Department for Education and Skills (UK). (2002). *Supporting early identification and intervention for children with special educational needs.* Retrieved January 27, 2008 from: http://www.standards.dfes.gov.uk/primary/publications/foundation_stage/1093763/

Department for Education and Skills (UK). (2003a). *Data collection by type of special educational need.* Retrieved January 24, 2008 from: https://czone.eastsussex.gov.uk/county_information/virtual_schoolbag/document.asp?item=1513

Department for Education and Skills (UK). (2003b). *Targeting support: Choosing and implementing interventions for children with significant learning difficulties.* Retrieved January 28, 2008 from: http://www.standards.dfes.gov.uk/primary/publications/literacy/63437/nls_chooseintervent_020103.pdf

Department for Education and Skills (UK). (2004). *Induction training for teaching assistants in secondary schools.* London: DfES.

Department of Education, Employment and Training (Vic.). (2001). *Middle years successful interventions literacy project.* Melbourne: Author.

Department of Education, Training and the Arts (Qld). (2006). Learning difficulties. Retrieved May 1, 2008 from: http://education.qld.gov.au/ studentservices/learning/learndiff/

Deschenes, C., Ebeling, D., & Sprague, J. (1999). *Adapting the curriculum in inclusive classrooms.* New York: National Professional Resources.

DEST (Department of Education, Science and Training, Australia). (2005). *Teaching Reading: National Inquiry into the Teaching of Literacy.* Canberra: Government Printing Service, Commonwealth of Australia.

Dettmer, P., Thurston, L., & Dyck, N. (2005). *Consultation, collaboration and teamwork for students with special needs* (5th ed.). Boston: Pearson-Allyn & Bacon.

Dettori, G., & Ott, M. (2006). Looking beyond the performance of grave under-achievement in mathematics. *Intervention in School and Clinic, 41, 4,* 201–208.

DfCSF (Department for Children, Schools and Families, UK). (2007). *Teaching numeracy.* TeacherNet: Department for Children, Schools and Families. Retrieved November 2, 2007 from: http://www.teachernet.gov.uk/ teachingandlearning/subjects/maths/teachingnumeracy/

Dickinson, P. (2003). Whole class interactive teaching. *SET Research for Teachers 1,* 18–21. Wellington: New Zealand Council for Educational Research.

Donahue, M. L., & Pearl, R. (2003). Studying social development and learning disabilities is not for the faint-hearted: Comments on the risk/resilience framework. *Learning Disabilities Research and Practice, 18, 2,* 90–93.

Doveston, M., & Keenaghan, M. (2006). Improving classroom dynamics to support students' learning and social inclusion: A collaborative approach. *Support for Learning 21, 1,* 5–11.

Dowker, A. (2004). *What works for children with mathematical difficulties? Research Report 554.* London: Department for Education and Skills. Retrieved January 28, 2008 from: http://www.dfes.gov.uk/research/data/uploadfiles/RR554.pdf

Eccles, J. S., Wigfield, A., & Schiefele, U. (1998). Motivation to succeed. In W. Damon & N. Eisenberg (Eds.), *Handbook of child psychology* (5th ed., vol. 3, pp. 1017–1095). New York: Wiley.

Edith Cowan University. (2007). *Overview of STEPS professional development course and resources.* Retrieved February 8, 2008 from: http://www.stepspd.com/au/ courses/index.asp

Elkins, J. (2000). All empires fall, you just have to know where to push. Antecedent issues for a study of learning difficulties in Australia. *Australian Journal of Learning Disabilities, 5, 2,* 4–7.

Elkins, J. (2007). Learning disabilities: Bringing fields and nations together. *Journal of Learning Disabilities, 40, 5,* 392–399.

Elksnin, L. K. (2002). Redefining LD is not the answer. In R. Bradley, L. Danielson, & D. P. Hallahan (Eds.), *Identification of learning disabilities: research to practice* (pp. 251–261). Mahwah, NJ: Erlbaum.

Elliott, J. G. (2008). The dyslexia myth. *Learning Difficulties Australia Bulletin, 40, 1,* 10–14.

Ellis, L. A. (2005). *Balancing approaches: Revisiting the educational psychology research on teaching students with learning difficulties.* Melbourne: Australian Council for Educational Research.

Erlbaum, B. (2002). The self-concept of students with disabilities: A meta-analysis of comparisons across different placements. *Learning Disabilities Research and Practice, 17, 4,* 216–226.

Fahsl, A. J. (2007). Mathematics accommodations for all students. *Intervention in School and Clinic, 42, 4,* 198–203.

Fielding-Barnsley, R., & Purdie, N. (2003). Early intervention in the home for children at risk of reading failure. *Support for Learning, 18, 2,* 77–82.

Firth, N. (2006). Success despite specific learning disabilities, *Australian Journal of Learning Disabilities, 11, 3,* 131–137.

Firth, N., Cunningham, E., & Skues, J. (2007). Primary and secondary perceived control: A comparison of adolescent students with and without learning disabilities. *Australian Journal of Learning Disabilities, 12, 1,* 11–17.

Fletcher-Campbell, F., Meijer, C. J. W., & Pijl, S. J. (1999). Integration policy and practice. In R. Bosker, B. P. M. Creemers & S. Stringfield (Eds.), *Enhancing educational excellence, equity and efficiency* (pp. 65–88). Dordrecht: Kluwer Academic.

Flynn, J. M., & Rahbar, M. (1998). Improving teacher prediction of children at risk of reading failure. *Psychology in the Schools, 35, 2,* 163–172.

Foorman, B. R., Schatschneider, C., Eakin, M. N., Fletcher, J. M., Moats, L. C., & Francis, D. J. (2006). The impact of instructional practices in Grades 1 and 2 on reading and spelling achievement in high poverty schools. *Contemporary Educational Psychology, 31, 1,* 1–29.

Forness, S., Kavale, K., Blum, I., & Lloyd, J. (1997). A mega-analysis of meta-analyses: What works in special education and related services? *Teaching Exceptional Children, 29, 6,* 4–7.

Fox, C. L., & Boulton, M. J. (2005). The social skills problems of victims of bullying: Self, peer and teacher perceptions. *British Journal of Educational Psychology, 75, 2,* 313–28.

Fox, G. (2003). *A handbook for learning support assistants* (2nd ed.). London: Fulton.

Frey, L. M., & Wilhite, K. (2005). Our five basic needs: Application for understanding the function of behaviour. *Intervention in School and Clinic, 40, 3,* 156–160.

Fried, S., & Fried, P. (2003). *Bullies, targets and witnesses.* New York: Evans.

Fry, J., & Bartak, L. (2006). Teachers' perceptions of the support needs of students with learning difficulties and emotional/behavioural disorders in mainstream primary and secondary schools. *Australian Journal of Dyslexia, 1, 1,* 24–30.

Fuchs, L., & Fuchs, D. (1998). General educators' instructional adaptations for students with learning disabilities. *Learning Disabilities Quarterly, 21,* 23–33.

Gage, N., & Berliner, D. (1998). *Educational psychology* (6th ed.). Boston: Houghton Mifflin.

Galbraith, A., & Alexander, J. (2005). Literacy, self-esteem, and locus of control. *Support for Learning, 20, 1,* 28–34.

Galletly, S. (1999). Making a lasting difference: The phonological + literacy combination. In P. Westwood, & W. Scott (Eds.), *Learning disabilities: Advocacy and action* (pp. 287–306). Melbourne: Australian Resource Educators' Association.

Gans, A.M., Kenny, M.C., & Ghany, D.L. (2003). Comparing the self-concept of students with and without learning disabilities. *Journal of Learning Disabilities, 36, 3,* 287–295.

Gersten, R., Jordan, N. C., & Flojo, J. R. (2005). Early identification and interventions for students with mathematics difficulties. *Journal of Learning Disabilities, 38, 4,* 293–304.

Goddard, A. (1995). From product to process in curriculum planning: A view from Britain. *Journal of Learning Disabilities, 28, 5,* 258–63.

Good, T. L., & Brophy, J. E. (2008). *Looking in classrooms* (10th ed.). Boston: Pearson-Allyn & Bacon.

Government of South Australia (2007). *South Australia's action plan for literacy and numeracy.* Council of Australian Governments. Retrieved January 27, 2008 from: http://www.premcab.sa.gov.au/pdf/coag/coag_ap_literacy.pdf

Graham, L., & Bailey, J. (2007). Learning disabilities and difficulties: An Australian conspectus. *Journal of Learning Disabilities, 40, 5,* 386–391.

Graham, L., Bellert, A., Thomas, J., & Pegg, J. (2007). QuickSmart: A basic academic skills intervention for middle school students with learning difficulties. *Journal of Learning Disabilities, 40, 5,* 410–419.

Greaves, D. (2000). Mapping the diversity of services and interventions for students with learning difficulties. *Australian Journal of Learning Disabilities, 5, 2,* 34–38.

Gresham, F. M. (2002). Social skills assessment and instruction for students with emotional and behavioral disorders. In K. L. Lane, F. M. Gresham, & T. E. O'Shaughnessy (Eds.), *Interventions for children with or at risk for emotional and behavioral disorders.* Boston, MA: Allyn & Bacon.

Hall, S. (1997). The problem with differentiation. *School Science Review, 78,* 284, 95–98.

Hallam, S. (1996). *Grouping pupils by ability: Selection, streaming, banding and setting.* London: Institute of Education.

Hallinan, P. , Hallinan, P., & Boulter, M. (1999). Enhancing student learning: Inclusion in practice at a Queensland high school. *Australian Journal of Learning Disabilities, 4, 1,* 10–13.

Hannavy, S. (1993). *Middle Infant Screening Test* (MIST). Windsor: NFER-Nelson.

Harlen, W., & Malcolm, H. (1997). *Setting and streaming: A research review.* Edinburgh: Scottish Council for Research in Education.

Harris, S., & Petrie, G. F. (2003). *Bullying: The bullies, the victims, and the bystanders.* Lanham: Scarecrow Press.

Hay, I., Elias, G., & Booker, G. (2005). Students with learning difficulties in relation to literacy and numeracy. *Schooling Issues Digest 2005/1.* Canberra: Department of Education, Science and Training. Retrieved January 25, 2008 from: http://www.dest.gov.au/sectors/school_education/publications_ resources/schooling_issues_digest/schooling_issues_digest_learning_ difficulties.htm

Heath, S. (2005). Why wait till children fail? Early screening for children at risk for reading problems. *Learning Difficulties Australia Bulletin, 37, 3,* 16–17.

Heiman, T. (2001). Depressive mood in students with mild intellectual disability: Students' reports and teachers' evaluations. *Journal of Intellectual Disability Research, 45, 6,* 526–534.

Hempenstall, K. (2005). The whole language–phonics controversy: A historical perspective. *Australian Journal of Learning Disabilities, 10, 3/4,* 19–33.

Heward, W. L. (2003). Ten faulty notions about teaching and learning that hinder the effectiveness of special education. *Journal of Special Education, 36, 4,* 186–205.

Hockenbury, J., Kauffman, J. M., & Hallahan, D. P. (2000). What is right about special education? *Exceptionality, 8, 1,* 3–11.

Hotchkis, G. D. (1999). Some existing impediments to attaining excellence in a new century. *Australasian Journal of Special Education, 22, 3,* 148–157.

Hudson, P. A. (2003). Behavioural intervention plan: Reducing challenging behaviour through academic skills instruction. *Special Education Perspectives, 12, 2,* 35–64.

Humphrey, N. (2002) Teacher and pupil ratings of self-esteem in developmental dyslexia. *British Journal of Special Education, 29, 1,* 29–36.

Hunt, P. (2004). Developing inclusive practices for delivering the curriculum at Singleton High School. *Special Education Perspectives, 13, 2,* 10–26.

Hutchinson, N. L., Freeman, J. G., & Bell, K. S. (2002). Children and adolescents with learning disabilities: Case studies of social relations in inclusive classrooms. In B. Y. L. Wong, & M. Donahue (Eds.), *The social dimensions of learning disabilities* (pp. 189–214). Mahwah, NJ: Erlbaum.

Iversen, S., Tunmer, W., & Chapman, J. W. (2005). The effects of varying group size on the Reading Recovery approach to preventive early intervention. *Journal of Learning Disabilities, 38, 5*, 456–72.

Janney, R., & Snell, M. E. (2004). *Modifying schoolwork* (2nd ed.). Baltimore: Brookes.

Johnson, D. W., & Johnson, F. P. (2003). *Joining together: Group theory and group skills* (8th ed.). Boston: Allyn & Bacon.

Johnston, R., & Watson, J. (2005). A seven years study of the effects of synthetic phonics teaching on reading and spelling attainment. *Insight 17.* Edinburgh: Scottish Executive Education Department.

Juel, C., Griffith, P., & Gough, P. (1986). Acquisition of literacy: A longitudinal study of children in first and second grade. *Journal of Educational Psychology, 78*, 243–255.

Karande, S., Sawant, S., Kulkarni, M., Kanchan, S., & Sholapurwala, R. (2005). Cognition in specific learning disabilities. *Indian Journal of Pediatrics, 72*, 1029–1033.

Kavale, K. A., & Forness, S. (1996). Social skills deficits and learning disabilities: A meta-analysis. *Journal of Learning Disabilities, 29*, 226–237.

Kavale, K. A., Holdnack, J. A., & Mostert, M. P. (2005). Responsiveness to intervention and the identification of specific learning disability: A critique and proposal. *Learning Disability Quarterly, 28*, 2–16.

Kavale, K. A., & Mostert, M. (2004). Social skills interventions for individuals with learning disabilities. *Learning Disability Quarterly 27, 1*, 31–43.

Kilpatrick, J., Swafford, J., & Findell, B. (2001). *Adding + it up: Helping children learn mathematics.* Washington, DC: National Academy Press.

Kirschner, P. A., Sweller, J., & Clark, R. E. (2006). Why minimal guidance during instruction does not work: An analysis of the failure of constructivist, discovery, problem-based, experiential and inquiry-based teaching. *Educational Psychologist, 4, 2*, 75–86.

Klassen, R. M., & Lynch, S. L. (2007). Self-efficacy from the perspective of adolescents with LD and their specialist teachers. *Journal of Learning Disabilities, 40, 6*, 494–507.

Klinger, J., & Vaughn, S. (1999). Students' perceptions of instruction in inclusive classrooms: Implications for students with learning disabilities. *Exceptional Children, 66, 1*, 23–37.

Knight, B. A., Graham, L., & Hughes, D. (2004). Facilitating positive social interaction for children with learning disabilities. In B. A. Knight, & W. Scott (Eds.), *Learning difficulties: Multiple perspectives* (pp. 171–185). Frenchs Forest, NSW: Pearson.

Kovacs, K. (1998). Preventing failure at school. *OECD Observer 214.* Retrieved January 21, 2008 from: http://www1.oecd.org/publications/observer/214/article2-eng.htm

Kroll, B. (1999). Social constructivist theory and its relationship to effective teaching of students with learning difficulties. In P. Westwood, & W. Scott (Eds.), *Learning disabilities: Advocacy and action* (pp. 21–28). Melbourne: Australian Resource Educators' Association.

Lancaster, J. (2005). Is it really possible? Can students with learning difficulties ever achieve higher levels of self-efficacy? *Special Education Perspectives, 14, 2,* 46–61.

Landerl, K., Bevan, A., & Butterworth, B. (2004). Developmental dyscalculia and basic numerical capacities: A study of 8–9 years old students. *Cognition, 93, 2,* 99–125.

LDonline Org. (2008). *Learning disabilities.* Retrieved January 22, 2008 from: http://www.ldonline.org/indepth/aboutld

Lerner, J., & Kline, F. (2006). *Learning disabilities and related disorders* (10th ed.). Boston: Houghton Mifflin.

Leung, C., Lindsay, G., & Lo, S. K. (2007). Early identification of primary school students with learning difficulties in Hong Kong: The development of a checklist. *European Journal of Special Needs Education, 22, 3,* 327–339.

Lewis, A. (1995). *Primary special needs and the National Curriculum.* London: Routledge.

Lewis, R. B., & Doorlag, D. H. (2006). *Teaching special students in general education classrooms* (7th ed.). Upper Saddle River, NJ: Pearson-Merrill-Prentice Hall.

Liddle, E., & Porath, M. (2002). Gifted children with written output difficulties: Paradox or paradigm? *Australian Journal of Learning Disabilities, 7, 2,* 13–19.

Lindberg, J. A., Kelley, D.E., & Swick, A. M. (2005). *Commonsense classroom management for middle and high school teachers.* Thousand Oaks, CA: Corwin Press.

Lloyd, S., & Wernham, S. (1995). *Jolly Phonics Workbooks.* Chigwell, Essex: Jolly Learning.

Logan, A. (2006). The role of the special needs assistant supporting pupils with special educational needs in Irish primary schools. *Support for Learning, 21, 2,* 92–99.

Louden, W., Chan, L., Elkins, J., Greaves, D., House, H., Milton, S., Nicols, S., Rohl, M., Rivalland, J., & van Kraayenoord, C. (2000). *Mapping the territory: Primary students with learning difficulties in literacy and numeracy.* Canberra: Department of Education, Training and Youth Affairs.

Lovett, B. J., & Lewandowski, L. J. (2006). Gifted students with learning disabilities: Who are they? *Journal of Learning Disabilities, 39, 6,* 515–527.

Lucangeli, D., & Cabrele, S. (2006). Mathematical difficulties and ADHD. *Exceptionality, 14, 1,* 53–62.

Maag, J. W. (2005). Social skills training for youth with emotional and behavioral disorders and learning disabilities: Problems, conclusions and suggestions. *Exceptionality, 13, 3*, 155–72.

McCowen, G. (1998). An evaluation of the theoretical positions that underpin explanations of the nature of learning and learning difficulties. *Australian Journal of Learning Disabilities, 3, 3*, 22–25.

McInerney, D. M., & McInerney, V. (2006). *Educational psychology: Constructing learning* (4th ed.). Frenchs Forest, NSW: Prentice Hall.

MacInnis, C., & Hemming, H. (1995). Linking the needs of students with learning disabilities to a whole language curriculum. *Journal of Learning Disabilities, 28, 9*, 535–44.

McIntyre, H., & Ireson, J. (2002). Within-class ability grouping: Placement of pupils in groups and self-concept. *British Educational Research Journal, 28, 2*, 249–263.

McKissock, C. (2001). The role of counselling in supporting adults with dyslexia. In M. Hunter-Carsch (Ed.), *Dyslexia: a psychosocial perspective* (pp. 245–253). London: Whurr.

McMaster, K. L., Fuchs, D., & Fuchs, L. S. (2006). Research on peer-assisted learning strategies: The promise and the limitations of peer-mediated instruction. *Reading and Writing Quarterly, 22, 1*, 5–25.

McNamara, E. (1994). The concept of motivation: An applied psychologist's perspective. *Educational and Child Psychology, 11, 2*: 6–15.

Margolis, H., & McCabe, P. (2003). Self-efficacy: A key to improving motivation of struggling learners. *Preventing School Failure, 47, 4*, 162–176.

Marston, D. (1996). A comparison of inclusion only, pull-out only, and combined service models for students with mild disabilities. *Journal of Special Education, 30, 2*, 121–32.

Martlew, M., & Hodson, J. (1991). Children with mild learning difficulties in an integrated and in a special school: Comparisons of behaviour, teasing and teachers' attitudes. *British Journal of Educational Psychology, 61*, 355–372.

Mastropieri, M. A., & Scruggs, T. E. (2002). *Effective instruction for special education* (3rd ed.). Austin, TX: ProEd.

Mastropieri, M. A., Scruggs, T. E., & Butcher, K. (1997). How effective is inquiry learning for students with mild disabilities? *Journal of Special Education, 31, 2*, 199–211.

Mayer, R. E. (2004). Should there be a three strikes rule against pure discovery learning? The case for guided methods of instruction. *American Psychologist, 59, 1*, 14–19.

Michaelson, M. T. (2007). An overview of dyscalculia: Methods for ascertaining and accommodating dyscalculic children in the classroom. *Australian Mathematics Teacher, 63, 3*, 17–22.

Milton, M. (2000). How do schools provide for children with learning difficulties in numeracy? *Australian Journal of Learning Disabilities, 5, 2,* 23–27.

Milton, M., & Lewis, E. (2005). Teaching gifted children with learning difficulties in writing. *Australian Journal of Learning Disabilities, 10, 2,* 79–88.

Mishna, F. (2003). Learning disabilities and bullying: Double jeopardy. *Journal of Learning Disabilities, 36, 4,* 336–347.

Moran, D. J. (2004). The need for research-based educational methods. In D. J. Moran, & R. W. Malott (Eds.), *Evidence-based educational methods* (pp. 3–7). San Diego, CA: Elsevier Academic.

Moriarty, B., Douglas, G., Punch, K., & Hattie, J. (1995). The importance of self-efficacy as a mediating variable between learning environments and achievement. *British Journal of Educational Psychology, 65,* 73–84.

Morrow, L. M., & Woo, D. G. (2001). *Tutoring programs for struggling readers.* New York: Guilford Press.

Munro, J. (2002). The reading characteristics of gifted learning disabled students. *Australian Journal of Learning Disabilities, 7, 2,* 4–12.

National Center for Learning Disabilities (US). (2001). *Learning disability.* Retrieved January 22, 2008 from: http://www.ncld.org/content/view/447/391/

National Council of Teachers of Mathematics (US). (2000). *Principles and standards for school mathematics.* Reston, VA: NCTM.

National Health and Medical Research Council. (1990). *Learning difficulties in children and adolescents.* Canberra: Australian Government Publishing Service.

National Institute for Literacy. (2008). *Learning disabilities.* Retrieved January 22, 2008 from: http://nifl.gov./nifl/facts/learning_disabilities.html

National Joint Committee on Learning Disabilities. (2006). *Learning disabilities and young children: Identification and intervention.* Retrieved January 22, 2008 from: http://www.ldonline.org/about/partners/njcld

National Reading Panel (US). (2000). *Teaching children to read: An evidence-based assessment of the scientific research literature on reading and its implications for reading instruction.* Washington, DC: National Institute of Child Health and Human Development.

Ng, L. (2006). *Annual monitoring of Reading Recovery: Data for 2004.* Wellington: New Zealand Ministry for Education.

Nicholson, T. (2006). How to avoid reading failure: Teach phonemic awareness. In McKeough, A., Lupart, J. L., Phillips, L. M., & Timmons, V. (Eds.), *Understanding literacy development: A global view.* Mahwah, NJ: Erlbaum.

Norwich, B., & Kelly, N. (2004). Pupils' views on inclusion: Moderate learning difficulties and bullying in mainstream and special schools. *British Educational Research Journal, 30, 1,* 43–65.

NSW Standing Committee on Social Issues. (2003). *Realising potential: Final report of the Inquiry into Early Intervention for Children with Learning Difficulties (Report 30).* Sydney: NSW Parliament.

Oakes, J. (1985). *Keeping track: How schools structure inequality.* New Haven: Yale University Press.

Oakes, J. (1994). Ability grouping and tracking in schools. In T. Husen, & T. N. Postlethwaite (Eds.), *The international encyclopedia of education* (2nd ed. vol. 1, pp. 6–12). Oxford: Pergamon.

O'Connor, E. A., & Simic, O. (2002). The effect of Reading Recovery on special education referrals and placements, *Psychology in the Schools, 39, 6,* 635–46.

OECD (Organisation for Economic Cooperation and Development). (1999). *Inclusive education at work: students with disabilities in mainstream schools.* Paris: OECD Centre for Educational Research and Innovation.

OECD (Organisation for Economic Cooperation and Development). (2000). *Special needs education: Statistics and indicators.* Paris: OECD Centre for Educational Research and Innovation.

OECD (Organisation for Economic Cooperation and Development). (2005). *Students with disabilities, learning difficulties and disadvantage: Statistics and indicators.* Paris: OECD.

Okabayashi, H. (1996). Intervention for school bullying: Observing American schools. *Psychologia, 39,* 163–178.

Ormrod, J. E. (2005). *Educational psychology: Developing learners* (5th ed.). Upper Saddle River, NJ: Pearson-Merrill.

Paas, F., Renkl, A., & Sweller, J. (2004). Cognitive load theory: Instructional implications of the interaction between information structures and cognitive architecture. *Instructional Science, 32,* 1–8.

Pajares, F., & Urdan, T. (Eds.), (2006). *Self-efficacy beliefs of adolescents.* Greenwich, CT: Information Age Publishing.

Parker, M., & Hurry, J. (2007). Teachers' use of questioning and modelling comprehension skills in primary schools. *Educational Review, 59, 3,* 299–314.

Pavri, S., & Monda-Amaya, L. (2001). Social support in inclusive schools: Student and teacher perspectives. *Exceptional Children, 67, 3,* 391–411.

Payne, T., & Irons, E. (2003). *Learning disability resource package.* Canberra: Commonwealth Government of Australia.

Pearce, S., Wheldall, K., & Madelaine, A. (2006). Multilit book levels: Towards a new system for leveling texts. *Special Education Perspectives, 15, 1,* 38–56.

Pearl, R., & Bay, M. (1999). Psychosocial correlates of learning disabilities. In V. L. Schwean & D. H. Saklofske (Eds.), *Handbook of psychosocial characteristics of exceptional children* (pp. 443–470). New York: Kluwer Academic.

Pierangelo, R., & Giuliani, G. (2006). *Learning disabilities: A practical approach to foundations, assessment, diagnosis and teaching.* Boston, MA: Pearson-Allyn & Bacon.

Pincott, R. (2004). Are we responsible for our children's maths difficulties? In B. A. Knight, & W. Scott (Eds.), *Learning difficulties: Multiple perspectives* (pp. 129–140). Frenchs Forest, NSW: Pearson.

Poulou, M. (2005). The prevention of emotional and behavioural difficulties in schools: Teachers' suggestions. *Educational Psychology in Practice, 21, 1*, 37–52.

Pressley, M. (2006). *Reading instruction that works: The case for balanced teaching* (3rd ed.). New York: Guilford Press.

Queensland Studies Authority. (2007). *Learning difficulties.* Retrieved January 21, 2008 from: http://www.qsa.qld.edu.au/downloads/syllabus/kla_special_needs_info_learning.pdf

Rappley, M. D. (2005). Attention-Deficit Hyperactivity Disorder. *New England Journal of Medicine, 352, 2*, 165–73.

Reading Recovery Council of North America. (2002). *What evidence says about Reading Recovery: Executive summary.* Columbus, OH: RRCNA.

Reddington, J. M., & Wheeldon, A. (2002). Involving parents in baseline assessment: Employing developmental psychopathology in the early identification process. *Dyslexia, 8, 2*, 119–122.

Riddick, B. (1996). *Living with dyslexia.* London: Routledge.

Riggs, J. (1999). The Einstein factor: Who advocates for the gifted learning disabled student in the classroom? In P. Westwood, & W. Scott (Eds.), *Learning disabilities: Advocacy and action* (pp. 241–251). Melbourne: Resource Educators' Association.

Riley, K. A., & Rustique-Forrester, E. (2002). *Working with disaffected students.* London: Paul Chapman.

Rivalland, J. (2000). Definitions and identification: Who are the children with learning difficulties? *Australian Journal of Learning Disabilities, 5, 2*, 4–7.

Robinson, G. (2002). Assessment of learning disabilities: The complexity of causes and consequences. *Australian Journal of Learning Disabilities, 7, 1*, 29–39.

Rohl, M. (2000). Programs and strategies used by teachers to support primary students with difficulties in learning literacy. *Australian Journal of Learning Disabilities, 5, 2*, 17–22.

Rose, J. (2006). *Independent review of the teaching of early reading.* London: Department of Education and Skills.

Rowe, H. (1981). *Early identification and intervention: A handbook for teachers and school counsellors.* Melbourne: Australian Council for Educational Research.

Rowe, K. (2006a). Effective teaching practices for students with and without learning difficulties: Issues and implications surrounding key findings and recommendations from the National Inquiry into the Teaching of Literacy. *Australian Journal of Learning Disabilities, 11, 3,* 99–115.

Rowe, K. (2006b). Effective teaching practices. *ACER e-News, 48,* 1–3.

Ryan, J., & Brown, M. (2005). Just for them to understand better: The impact of learning difficulties at university. *Australian Journal of Learning Disabilities, 10, 1,* 19–24.

Santrock, J. W. (2006). *Life-span development* (10th ed.). Boston: McGraw Hill.

Schumm, J. S., & Vaughn, S. (1995). Getting ready for inclusion: Is the stage set? *Learning Disabilities Research and Practice, 10, 3,* 169–179.

Scruggs, T. E., & Mastropieri, M. A. (2007). Science learning in special education: The case for constructed versus instructed learning. *Exceptionality, 15, 2,* 57–74.

Seevers, R. L., & Jones-Blank, M. (2008). Exploring the effects of social skills training on student behaviour. *National Forum of Special Education Journal, 19, 1,* 1–8.

Seligman, M. E. P. (1995). *The optimistic child.* Boston: Houghton Mifflin.

Selikowitz, M. (1998). *Dyslexia and other learning difficulties* (2nd ed.). Oxford: Oxford University Press.

Shaddock, T. (2006). *Researching effective teaching and learning practices for students with learning difficulties and disabilities in the Australian Capital Territory: Final Report.* Canberra: Commonwealth Government of Australia.

Shanahan, J., & Richmond, C. (2007). Behaviour management via single case intervention. *Special Education Perspective, 16, 2,* 5–19.

Sideridis, G. (2007). Why are students with LD depressed? A goal orientation model of depression vulnerability. *Journal of Learning Disabilities, 40, 6,* 526–539.

Sideridis, G., & Greenwood, C. (1998). Identification and validation of effective instructional practices for children from impoverished backgrounds and those with learning and developmental disabilities using ecobehavioural analysis. *European Journal of Special Needs Education, 13, 2,* 145–154.

Siegel, L., & Brayne, R. (2005). *Early identification and intervention to prevent reading difficulties.* CMEC Toronto. Retrieved January 28, 2008 from: http://www.edu.gov.on.ca/eng/literacynumeracy/inspire/pdfs/F2.pdf

Slavin, R. E. (1994). Preventing early school failure. In R. E. Slavin, N. L. Karweit, & B. A. Wasik (Eds.), *Preventing early school failure* (pp. 1–12). Boston: Allyn & Bacon.

Slavin, R. E. (2004). Built to last: Long-term maintenance of 'Success for All'. *Remedial and Special Education 25, 1,* 61–66.

Slavin, R. E., & Madden, N. A. (2001). *One million children: Success for All.* Thousand Oaks, CA: Corwin Press.

Sloat, E. A., Beswick, J. F., & Willms, J. D. (2007). Using early literacy monitoring to prevent reading failure. *Phi Delta Kappan, 88, 7,* 523–529.

Smart, D., Prior, M., Sanson, A., & Oberklaid, F. (2001). Children with reading difficulties: A six-year follow-up from early primary to secondary school. *Australian Journal of Psychology, 53, 1*, 45–53.

Smidt, S. (2002). *A guide to early years practice* (2nd ed.). London: Routledge.

Smith-Burke, M. T. (2001). Reading Recovery: A systematic approach to early intervention. In L. M. Morrow and D. G. Woo (Eds.), *Tutoring programs for struggling readers*. New York: Guilford Press.

Stephenson, J. (2006). Behavioural momentum: A practical antecedent strategy to reduce noncompliance. *Special Education Perspectives, 15, 2*, 40–47.

Stewart, W. (2002). Electronic assistive technology for the gifted and learning-disabled student. *Australian Journal of Learning Disabilities, 7, 4*, 4–12.

Stigler, J. W., & Hiebert, J. (2004). Improving maths teaching. *Educational Leadership, 61, 5*, 12–17.

Sugai, G., & Evans, D. (1997). Using teachers' perceptions to screen for primary students with high-risk behaviours. *Australasian Journal of Special Education, 21, 1*, 18–35.

Swanson, H. L. (1999). *Interventions for students with learning disabilities: Meta-analysis of treatment outcomes*. New York: Guilford Press.

Swanson, H. L. (2000). What instruction works for students with learning disabilities? In R. Gersten, E. Schiller, & S. Vaughn (Eds.), *Contemporary special education research* (pp. 1–30). Mahwah, NJ: Erlbaum.

Swanson, H. L., & Deshler, D. (2003). Instruction for adolescents with learning disabilities: Converting a meta-analysis to practice. *Journal of Learning Disabilities, 36, 2*, 124–134.

Symons, A., & Greaves, D. (2006). The use of the THRASS program with younger children with literacy difficulties. *Australian Journal of Dyslexia, 1, 1*, 31–36.

Tait, K. (2007). Problem behaviour or just a communication breakdown? *Special Education Perspectives, 16, 1*, 10–17.

Tennant, G. (2007). IEPs in mainstream secondary schools: An agenda for research. *Support for Learning, 22, 4*, 204–208.

Tollefson, J. M., Mellard, D. F., & McKnight, M. A. (2007). Responsiveness to intervention: A SLD determination resource. National Research Center on Learning Disabilities, *Information Digest* (Winter issue 2007). Retrieved January 28, 2008 from: http://www.nrcld.org/resource_kit/general/RTIdigest2007.pdf

Tomlinson, C. A. (1996). *Differentiating instruction for mixed-ability classrooms*. Alexandria, VA: Association for Supervision and Curriculum.

Tomlinson, C. A. (2001). *How to differentiate instruction in mixed-ability classrooms* (2nd ed.). Alexandria, VA: Association for Supervision and Curriculum Development.

Torgesen, J. K. (2002). The prevention of reading difficulties. *Journal of School Psychology, 40, 1*, 7–26.

Tur-Kaspa, H. (2002). Social cognition in learning disabilities. In B. Y. L. Wong, & M. Donahue. *The social dimensions of learning disabilities* (pp. 11–31). Mahwah, NJ: Erlbaum.

Twaddle, P. (2001). If you want to make a difference, intervene: The Australian Kindergarten Screening Instrument. *Australian Journal of Learning Disabilities, 6, 4,* 26–35.

Twomey, E. (2006). Linking learning theories and learning difficulties. *Australian Journal of Learning Disabilities, 11, 2,* 93–98.

US Department of Education. (2004). *Individuals with Disabilities Education Act* (IDEA). Retrieved January 30, 2008 from: http://idea.ed.gov

Valas, H. (1999). Students with learning disabilities and low-achieving students: Peer acceptance, loneliness, self-esteem and depression. *Social Psychology of Education, 3,* 173–192.

Valas, H. (2001). Learned helplessness and psychological adjustment: Effects of learning disabilities and low achievement. *Scandinavian Journal of Educational Research, 45, 2,* 101–114.

van den Berg, R., Sleegers, P., & Geijsel, F. (2001). Teachers' concerns about adaptive teaching: Evaluation of a support program. *Journal of Curriculum and Supervision, 16, 3,* 245–258.

Vaughn, S., Gersten, R., & Chard, D. J. (2000). The underlying message in LD intervention research: Findings from research syntheses. *Exceptional Children, 67, 1,* 99–114.

Vaughn, S., Zartagoza, N., Hogan, A., & Walker, J. (1993). A four-year longitudinal investigation of the social skills and behaviour problems of students with learning disabilities. *Journal of Learning Disabilities, 26,* 404–412.

Vlachou, A., Didaskalou, E., & Argyrakouli, E. (2006). Preferences of students with general learning difficulties for different service delivery modes. *European Journal of Special Needs Education, 21, 2,* 201–216.

Wain, G. (1994). Mathematics education and society. In A. Orton, & G. Wain (Eds.), *Issues in teaching mathematics* (pp. 21–34). London: Cassell.

Wang, M. C. (1998). Serving students with special needs: What works and what does not. In D. W. Chan (Ed.), *Helping students with learning difficulties* (pp. 161–173). Hong Kong: Chinese University Press.

Wasik, B. A., & Karweit, N. L. (1994). Off to a good start: Effects of birth to three interventions on early school success. In R. E. Slavin, N. L. Karweit, & B. A. Wasik (Eds.), *Preventing early school failure.* Boston: Allyn & Bacon.

Watson, J. (2005). *The school experience of secondary students with learning difficulties: The marriage of quantitative and qualitative data.* Paper presented at the International Educational Research Conference, UWS, Parramatta, 27 November to 1 December 2005.

Watson, J., & Boman, P. (2005). Mainstream students with learning difficulties: Failing and underachieving in the secondary school. *Australian Journal of Learning Disabilities, 10, 2,* 43–49.

Watson, J., & Bond, T. G. (2007). Walking the walk: Rasch analysis of an exploratory survey of secondary teachers' attitudes and understanding of students with learning difficulties. *Australian Journal of Learning Disabilities, 12, 1,* 1–9.

Wearmouth, J. (2002). The role of the learning support coordinator: Addressing the challenges. In G. Reid, & J. Wearmouth (Eds.), *Dyslexia and literacy* (pp. 213–228). Chichester: Wiley.

Webber, L. S., Owens, J., Charlton, J. L., & Kershaw, M. M. (2002). Case studies in learning disabilities: Implications for instruction. *Australian Journal of Learning Disabilities, 7, 4,* 28–33.

Wendon, L. (2006). *Letterland.* Barton, Cambridge; Letterland International. Retrieved January 28, 2008 from: http://www.letterland.com/Teachers/Teachers_1.html

West, J. (2002). Motivation and access to help: The influence of status on one child's motivation for literacy learning. *Reading and Writing Quarterly, 18,* 205–229.

Westwood, P. (1995). Teachers' beliefs and expectations concerning students with learning difficulties. *Australian Journal of Remedial Education, 27, 2,* 19–21.

Westwood, P. (2006). *Teaching and learning difficulties.* Melbourne: Australian Council for Educational Research.

Westwood, P. (2008a). *What teachers need to know about reading and writing difficulties.* Melbourne: Australian Council for Educational Research.

Westwood, P. (2008b). *What teachers need to know about teaching methods.* Melbourne: Australian Council for Educational Research.

Westwood, P., & Graham, L. (2000). How many children with special needs in regular classes? Official predictions vs teachers' perceptions in South Australia and New South Wales. *Australian Journal of Learning Disabilities, 5, 2,* 24–34.

Whedon, C. K., & Bakken, J. P. (1999). Using the clock, light, radio technique to improve engaged time-on-task for students with learning disabilities. *Australian Journal of Learning Disabilities, 4, 2,* 6–10.

Wheldall, K. (2007). Efficacy of educational programs and interventions. *Learning Difficulties Australia Bulletin, 39, 1,* 3–4.

Wheldall, K., & Beaman, R. (2007). *Multilit tutor program (revised).* Sydney: Macquarie University.

Wheldall, K., & Byers, S. (2005). Submission from Learning Difficulties Australia to the National Inquiry into the Teaching of Literacy. *Australian Journal of Learning Disabilities, 10, 3/4,* 9–10.

Wiener, J. (2004). Do peer relationships foster behavioral adjustment in children with learning disabilities? *Learning Disability Quarterly, 27, 1,* 21–30.

Wilen, W., Ishler, M., Hutchison, J., & Kindsvatter, R. (2000). *Dynamics of effective teaching* (4th ed.). New York: Longman.

Wright, C. (2007). Increasing academic output in students with ADHD. *Learning Difficulties Australia Bulletin, 39, 4*, 11–12.

Wright, R. (2003). Mathematics Recovery: A program of intervention in early number learning. *Australian Journal of Learning Disabilities, 8, 4*, 6–11.

Yamanashi, J. E. (2005). A cooperative approach to assisting students at risk of educational failure. *Special Education Perspectives, 14, 2*, 62–76.

Yuen, M. T., Westwood, P., & Wong, G. (2007). Bullying and social adjustment in a sample of Chinese students with specific learning disability. *Special Education Perspectives, 16, 2*, 35–52.

Zafiriadis, K. Luvaditis, M., Xenitidis, K. Diamonti, M., Tsatalmpasidou, E., Sigalas, I., & Polemitos, N. (2005). Social and psychological characteristics of Greek secondary school students with learning difficulties. *Journal of Adolescence, 28*, 741–752.

Zimmerman, T. (2007). Recognition and response. *Early Developments: Research-based Practice, 11, 1*, 6–10.

Zundans, L. (2003). Life narrative of a secondary school student with learning difficulties. *Australian Journal of Learning Disabilities, 8, 3*, 22–25.

Index

Main entries in **bold**